HIROSHIMA: THE DECISION TO USE THE A-BOMB

Martin Steinmann, Jr., GENERAL EDITOR

EDWIN FOGELMAN
University of Minnesota

HIROSHIMA: THE DECISION TO USE THE A-BOMB

CHARLES SCRIBNER'S SONS New York

A-8.64[H]

Printed in the United States of America
Library of Congress Catalog Card Number 64-21291

For MY BROTHER SI

IN MEMORIAM, 1922-1944

Death wins the field with ease,
But falters driving home his gain.

Preface

Each Scribner Research Anthology is a collection of written sources upon a single historical, political, literary, or scientific topic or problem—the Hungarian Revolt, Shakespeare's *Julius Cæsar,* or extrasensory perception, for example. In addition to these sources, it contains (1) "Guide to Research," an account of the rationale and the methods of research and of research-paper writing, (2) an introduction to the topic of the anthology, (3) suggested topics for controlled research, and (4) suggested sources and topics for library research.

Each anthology is designed to serve two purposes. First, each gives the student access to important sources—texts, documents, letters, diaries, essays, articles, reports, transcripts of hearings, for instance—on a given topic. Some of these sources are otherwise available in only a few libraries, some (manuscripts and historical and government documents) in only one. In any case, the collection as a whole is not otherwise available in one volume. Second, each anthology gives the student either all his sources for a controlled-research paper or some of them for a library-research paper. Each anthology can be valuable either for readings in courses in history, literature, science, or humanities or as the basis for a research paper in these or in other courses.

A controlled-research paper—a paper in which the student's search for sources is limited to, and in certain ways controlled by, those sources contained in one anthology—is not so noble an undertaking as a library-research paper. But it is often more successful—more rewarding for the student and easier for his instructor to teach effectively and judge fairly. Its advantages for both student and instructor are often considerable.

For the student, it sometimes provides sources unavailable in his school library. And it enables him to learn a good deal about research (selection, interpretation, and evaluation of sources; quotation and paraphrase; and documentation) without prior instruction in use of the library (and, incidentally, without overtaxing the facilities and the resources of his library and without loss of, or damage to, sources either irreplaceable or difficult and expensive to replace).

For the instructor, it permits focus of class discussion upon a limited set of topics. It enables him to track down the student's sources conveniently. And—perhaps the greatest advantage of all—it enables him to judge both conveniently and exactly how well the student has selected, interpreted, and evaluated his sources and how well he has quoted and paraphrased them.

In many schools, a controlled-research paper is either a preliminary to or a part of a library-research paper. A library-research paper is probably the most difficult paper that the student can be assigned to write. The problems that confront him are not simply those common to any paper—organization, paragraphing, and transitions, for instance—and those (already mentioned) common to all research papers. He has, in addition, the problem of using the library well—of, for example, using the card catalogue, periodical indexes, and other reference works. But, if the instructor assigns a controlled-research paper as a preliminary to or, as it were, an early part of a library-research paper, the student need not come to grips with all these problems at once.

Each Scribner Research Anthology is compiled according to the following editorial principles. Each source that is not anonymous is prefaced by a biographical note on its author. At the foot of the same page is a bibliographical note. Each source is reprinted exactly as it appears in the original except for (1) some typographical peculiarities, (2) explanatory notes, given in brackets, and (3) omissions, indicated by ellipses (". . ."). And, finally, for each source that has pagination in the original, page numbers are given in brackets within the source itself—thus: "[**320/321**]," where everything before the slash (and after the preceding slash, if any) is from page 320, and everything after the slash (and before the next slash, if any) is from page 321. For a source hitherto unpublished, no page numbers are given; and the student who uses it should cite the page numbers of the Scribner Research Anthology. Footnotes to a source are given as in the original. Where the original pagination of a footnote is not evident, its page number precedes it in brackets.

MARTIN STEINMANN, JR.

Bingham Bay
Lake Gogebic
August, 1960

Foreword

On first seeing the Scribner Research Anthologies prepared for use in English courses, I at once realized that here was a teaching device equally useful in political science courses. Consequently, I take satisfaction and pride in pointing out the virtues of these controlled-research books to other teachers of political science.

We who teach political science generally require students to do a paper involving research. To some degree, we are all, as Professor Steinmann suggests, confronted with the problems of limited library resources, with students who are unprepared for difficult research projects, and with the difficulty of fairly grading papers based upon sources not conveniently available. My own experience suggests that, when we assign research papers, we spend an inordinate amount of time with individual students answering questions about methods of research and research writing at the expense of discussion of the subject. Here we can with confidence refer the student to the "Guide to Research" for brief and detailed instructions on research and on writing papers and thus redress the balance and use precious conference time for discussion of the subject.

These anthologies may be employed effectively in another way. As we sweep through the subject matter of the beginning courses, our students often become interested in specific problems which they would like to explore more fully. Not yet knowledgeable in the ways of exploring the pros and cons of an issue, it is common for them to go to one easily available source and assume that they are getting full coverage. These anthologies can be used to demonstrate how one must go about researching a problem so that a number of points of view are examined. Toward that end, students could be required to read an anthology without writing a paper. Student understanding could be developed by classroom discussion and tested by oral reports and written examinations.

Third, these anthologies can be used as can any other supplementary book of readings on important and timely subjects in political science. Each anthology presents a balanced variety of views and lets the students draw their own conclusions, while preparing them to do superior work in selected topics requiring greater sophistication in research.

Although the topic of each volume is in political science, no volume assumes that the student has specialized knowledge of this science; and each volume may, therefore, be used in other courses—freshman English, for example.

HAROLD W. CHASE

University of Minnesota

Contents

Part Four: THE BOMBING OF HIROSHIMA IN PERSPECTIVE

HIROSHIMA: THE DECISION TO USE THE A-BOMB

Introduction

The decision to inaugurate the nuclear age by dropping an atomic bomb on the city of Hiroshima was one of the momentous acts of our time. To this day the wisdom of that decision is still a subject of controversy. One hundred and forty thousand people were condemned to death or injury on the bright morning of August 6, 1945. In restrospect there are serious questions as to whether the devastation was justified.

The work of building an atomic bomb was begun during World War II because of fear that the Germans were developing such a weapon for use against the Allies. From the outset it was clear that whoever first succeeded in producing atomic bombs would win the war. Later we learned that German scientists never actually attempted to produce an A-bomb, primarily because they believed that production of one was impossible, but during the war the menace seemed real and critical. By the time the war with Germany ended we had invested well over one billion dollars in the development of an atomic bomb—the final cost of the two bombs dropped on Hiroshima and Nagasaki was about two billion dollars—but had produced no bomb.

Since we were still at war with Japan, work on the bomb continued. Although there was no danger that the Japanese were developing such a weapon, the prospect of ending the war quickly by one overwhelming atomic attack spurred the scientists, technicians, and military personnel connected with the atomic project (centered in Los Alamos, New Mexico) to intensify their efforts. The goal was to produce an atomic bomb as soon as possible regardless of cost. Despite the doubts of critics, who believed the bomb would never work, the extraordinary enterprise proved successful beyond expectations.

But, as the moment of success drew closer, people began to ask how and even whether the unprecedented weapon should be used. This discussion was confined to a handful of men; for under prevailing conditions of secrecy only about a dozen men—high government officials, military advisers, and scientists—were involved in the awesome decision of whether and where the bomb would be dropped. Indeed, the secret of the bomb was so closely guarded that even Vice-President Truman had no knowledge of such a weapon until he succeeded to the presidency, on April 12, 1945. As soon as he learned about the weapon, President Truman appointed a special Interim Committee under the chairmanship of Secretary of War Henry L. Stimson, together with an advisory panel of distinguished scientists, to help him reach a final decision on its use. The recommendations of this committee and above all the advice of Secretary of War Stimson confirmed President Truman's own conviction that use of an atomic bomb against Japan would be necessary to bring the war to a speedy end.

The successful testing of an atomic bomb at Alamogordo, New Mexico, on July 17, 1945 coincided with the historic international conference held at Potsdam, Germany, among President Truman, Prime Minister Churchill, and Marshal Stalin. By the time of the Potsdam Conference Japan had suffered severe defeats from American naval and air forces. Japanese representatives had already approached the Russians, who were still neutral in the war against Japan, in an attempt to negotiate an end to the conflict. These and other Japanese attempts to negotiate met with no success, and in fact the Russians had promised a year earlier to join the Allies in their struggle against Japan. In those earlier days the intervention of Russia had been sought by the Allies as a means of insuring victory in the Pacific; now, with an atomic weapon in our possession and with growing strains in Russio-American relations, the need for such intervention seemed less vital.

So far as the bombing of Hiroshima is concerned, the most important aspect of the Potsdam Conference is the contents of the declaration issued to the Japanese from Potsdam by the United States, Great Britain, and China as an ultimatum to surrender. Two features of this Potsdam Declaration are especially controversial: first, the absence of explicit mention of the new atomic weapon; and, second, the absence of an explicit guarantee that the Japanese Imperial system would be preserved. Critics of the declaration have maintained that, if the Japanese leaders had been specifically warned about the impending atomic attack and if they had been assured that their emperor would remain on his throne during the occupation, then surrender would have followed without the bombing of Hiroshima and Nagasaki. The declaration did warn that "The alternative for Japan is prompt and utter destruction," but it did not speak either of atomic weapons or of the safety of the emperor. As it happened, the Japanese appeared to reject the Potsdam Declaration, and the fate of Hiroshima was sealed.

The selections that follow are divided into four sections.

The first section contains statements by some of the men who participated in the decision to bomb Hiroshima. These statements will help you to understand the objectives of these men, their estimate of the existing international situation, and their evaluation of the possible alternatives. You will notice that, although these men substantially agreed that the bomb must be used as a secret military weapon, some dissented strongly.

The second section contains statements by eminent scientists who designed and built the bomb. Some of these scientists were among the first to recognize the long-range moral and political implications of atomic warfare, although so long as the war continued the scientists overwhelmingly approved the use of their creation against Japan. Because of the secrecy surrounding the entire atomic project, the views of these scientists are especially important, since at the time these views were the only available expression of public opinion.

The third section contains statements of or on Japanese reaction to the bombing of Hiroshima. During the months preceding the attack the Japanese leaders seriously disagreed concerning the need for peace and the conditions on which surrender would be acceptable. The ultimate justification for the bombing of Hiroshima was that it helped bring World War II to a prompt end and thereby spared millions of casualties on both sides. There can be no doubt that the bombing did hasten the Japanese surrender. But the question remains whether Japan would not have surrendered very soon even without the atomic attack. Although no definitive answer is possible, the selections in this section will help you to reach some judgment of your own.

Finally, the fourth section contains postwar statements evaluating the bombing of Hiroshima. Karl Compton presents a case *for* the bombing; Hanson Baldwin, a case *against;* P.M.S. Blackett suggests a controversial diplomatic explanation of the bombing; and Robert Batchelder discusses the moral issues which our use of the bomb unavoidably raises.

Looking back across the crowded and dangerous years since the end of World War II, and considering the superweapons which now threaten all mankind, you may feel that the bombing of Hiroshima is a remote event without direct significance for us in the present. Yet the issues involved in the decision to bomb Hiroshima are as vital and relevant today as they were in 1945. Someday a president of the United States may face a decision very similar to that which President Truman faced in the closing days of World War II. Probably the city will not be Hiroshima, but the calculations and the pressures will be comparable.

Keeping in mind the possibility that a future president may find it necessary to decide, perhaps in the space of hours or even minutes, whether to order the devastation of cities many times larger than Hiroshima, you might ask yourself a number of questions that seem to occur as one reads the selections in this anthology. Were our decision-makers sufficiently aware of the political and the moral as opposed to the military significance of their decision? Did they permit a full hearing of all points of view before reaching their decision? Did they have adequate information about the enemy's military position and the intentions of the enemy's leaders? Did they make the best use of whatever information was available? No doubt these are difficult questions to answer, but they go to the heart of the sometimes agonizing process of making policy.

President Truman has assumed full personal responsibility for the decision to bomb Hiroshima. But there is a sense in which the decision was not really his. As you read the selections that follow, you may come to feel that from one point of view events were in the saddle riding mankind, that President Truman and almost everyone else connected with the decision merely responded to the momentum of developments over which they had little direct control. Wealth measured in sums of billions of dollars, the energies of thousands of individuals, attitudes that had been firmly held for years, unintentional and accidental circumstances—all these played a part in the bombing of Hiroshima quite apart from the thoughtful actions of particular men. Indeed, from this point of view arises the sobering question of whether the president could have decided *not* to bomb Hiroshima: perhaps in the context of the time such a decision would have been, as the historian Herbert Feis says, "a most resolute and courageous act of will—of a kind rarely recorded in history."[1] It is tempting to speculate whether such a historic act of will will ever be required in the future, and if so whether it will in fact be forthcoming.

[1] Herbert Feis, *Japan Subdued* (Princeton: Princeton University Press, 1961), p. 108.

PART ONE
THE DECISION-MAKERS

*Year of Decisions**

HARRY S TRUMAN (1884-   ) succeeded as thirty-third president of the United States on April 12, 1945, following the death of Franklin D. Roosevelt. The atomic bomb was dropped on Hiroshima on August 6, 1945, less than four months later. Before he became president, Mr. Truman held a variety of public offices, ranging from county judge to senator from Missouri and vice-president of the United States. At the time of his inauguration Mr. Truman knew nothing about the long-standing atomic energy program or about plans for the use of atomic bombs against Japan. Nevertheless, as president he accepted full responsibility for the decision to bomb Hiroshima.

The historic message of the first explosion of an atomic bomb was flashed to me in a message from Secretary of War Stimson on the morning of July 16. The most secret and the most daring enterprise of the war had succeeded. We were now in possession of a weapon that would not only revolutionize war but could alter the course of history and civilization. This news reached me at Potsdam the day after I had arrived for the conference of the Big Three.

Preparations were being rushed for the test atomic explosion at Alamogordo, New Mexico, at the time I had to leave for Europe, and on the voyage over I had been anxiously awaiting word on the results. I had been told of many predictions by the scientists, but no one was certain of the outcome of this full-scale atomic explosion. As I read the message from Stimson, I realized that the test not only met the most optimistic expectation of the scientists but that the United States had in its possession an explosive force of unparalleled power.

Stimson flew to Potsdam the next day to see me and brought with him the full details of the test. I received him at once and called in Secretary of State Byrnes, Admiral Leahy, General Marshall, General Arnold, and Admiral King to join us at my office at the Little White House. We reviewed our military strategy in the light of this revolutionary development. We were not ready to make use of this weapon against the Japanese, although we did not know as yet what effect the new weapon might have, physically or psychologically, when used against the enemy. For that reason the military advised that we go ahead with the existing military plans for the invasion of the Japanese home islands. [**415/416**]

At Potsdam, as elsewhere, the secret of the atomic bomb was kept closely guarded. We did not extend the very small circle of Americans who knew about it. Churchill naturally knew about the atomic bomb project from its very beginning, because it had involved the pooling of British and American technical skill.

On July 24 I casually mentioned to Stalin that we had a new weapon of unusual destructive force. The Russian Premier showed no special interest. All he said was that he was glad to hear it and hoped we would make "good use of it against the Japanese."

* Harry S Truman, from *Memoirs*, Vol. I: *Year of Decisions* (Garden City: Doubleday and Co., 1955), pp. 415-421.

A month before the test explosion of the atomic bomb the service Secretaries and the Joint Chiefs of Staff had laid their detailed plans for the defeat of Japan before me for approval. There had apparently been some differences of opinion as to the best route to be followed, but these had evidently been reconciled, for when General Marshall had presented his plan for a two-phase invasion of Japan, Admiral King and General Arnold had supported the proposal heartily.

The Army plan envisaged an amphibious landing in the fall of 1945 on the island of Kyushu, the southernmost of the Japanese home islands. This would be accomplished by our Sixth Army, under the command of General Walter Krueger. The first landing would then be followed approximately four months later by a second great invasion, which would be carried out by our Eighth and Tenth Armies, followed by the First Army transferred from Europe, all of which would go ashore in the Kanto plains area near Tokyo. In all, it had been estimated that it would require until the late fall of 1946 to bring Japan to her knees.

This was a formidable conception, and all of us realized fully that the fighting would be fierce and the losses heavy. But it was hoped that some of Japan's forces would continue to be preoccupied in China and others would be prevented from reinforcing the home islands if Russia were to enter the war.

There was, of course, always the possibility that the Japanese might choose to surrender sooner. Our air and fleet units had begun to inflict heavy damage on industrial and urban sites in Japan proper. Except in China, the armies of the Mikado had been pushed back everywhere in relentless successions of defeats.

Acting Secretary of State Grew had spoken to me in late May about issuing a proclamation that would urge the Japanese to surrender but would assure them that we would permit the Emperor to remain as head of the state. Grew backed this with arguments taken from his ten years' experience as our Ambassador in Japan, and I told him that I had already given thought to this matter myself and that it seemed to me a sound idea. Grew had a draft of a proclamation with him, and I instructed him to [**416/417**] send it by the customary channels to the Joint Chiefs and the State-War-Navy Co-ordinating Committee in order that we might get the opinions of all concerned before I made my decision.

On June 18 Grew reported that the proposal had met with the approval of his Cabinet colleagues and of the Joint Chiefs. The military leaders also discussed the subject with me when they reported the same day. Grew, however, favored issuing the proclamation at once, to coincide with the closing of the campaign on Okinawa, while the service chiefs were of the opinion that we should wait until we were ready to follow a Japanese refusal with the actual assault of our invasion forces.

It was my decision then that the proclamation to Japan should be issued from the forthcoming conference at Potsdam. This, I believed, would clearly demonstrate to Japan and to the world that the Allies were united in their purpose. By that time, also, we might know more about two matters of significance for our future effort: the participation of the Soviet Union and the atomic bomb. We knew that the bomb would receive its first test in mid-July. If the test of the bomb was successful, I wanted to afford Japan a clear chance to end the fighting before we made use of this newly gained power. If the test should fail, then it would be even more important to us to bring about a surrender before we had to make a physical conquest of Japan. General Marshall told me that it might cost half a million American lives to force the enemy's surrender on his home grounds.

But the test was now successful. The entire development of the atomic bomb had been dictated by military considerations. The idea of the atomic bomb had been suggested to President Roosevelt by the famous and brilliant Dr. Albert Einstein, and its development turned out to be a vast undertaking. It was the achievement of the combined efforts of science, industry, labor, and the military, and it had no parallel in history. The men in charge and their staffs worked under extremely high pressure, and the whole enormous task required the services of more than one hundred thousand men and immense quantities of material. It required over two and a half years and necessitated the expenditure of two and a half billions of dollars.

Only a handful of the thousands of men who worked in these plants knew what they were producing. So strict was the secrecy imposed that even some of the highest-ranking officials in Washington had not the slightest idea of what was going on. I did not. Before 1939 it had been generally agreed among scientists that it was theoretically possible to release energy from the atom. In 1940 we had begun to pool with Great Britain all scientific knowledge useful to war, although Britain was at war at that time and we were not. Following this—in 1942—we learned that [**417/418**] the Germans were at work on a method to harness atomic energy for use as a weapon of war. This, we understood, was to be added to the V-1 and V-2 rockets with which they hoped to conquer the world. They failed, of course, and for this we can thank Providence. But now a race was on to make the atomic bomb—a race that became "the battle of the laboratories."

It was under the general policy of pooling knowledge between our nation and Great Britain that research on the atomic bomb started in such feverish secrecy. American and British scientists joined in the race against the Germans. We in America had available a great number of distinguished scientists in many related fields of knowledge, and we also had another great advantage. We could provide the tremendous industrial and economic resources required for the project—a vastly expensive project—without injury to our war production program. Furthermore, our plants were far removed from the reach of enemy bombing. Britain, whose scientists had initiated the project and were contributing much of the original atomic data, was constantly exposed to enemy bombing and, when she started the atomic research, also faced the possibilty of invasion.

For these reasons Roosevelt and Churchill agreed to pool the research and concentrate all of the work on the development of the project within the United States. Working together with the British, we thus made it possible to achieve a great scientific triumph in the field of atomic energy. Nevertheless, basic and historic as this event was, it had to be considered at the time as relatively incidental to the far-flung war we were fighting in the Pacific at terrible cost in American lives.

We could hope for a miracle, but the daily tragedy of a bitter war crowded in on us. We labored to construct a weapon of such overpowering force that the enemy could be forced to yield swiftly once we could resort to it. This was the primary aim of our secret and vast effort. But we also had to carry out the enormous effort of our basic and traditional military plans.

The task of creating the atomic bomb had been entrusted to a special unit of the Army Corps of Engineers, the so-called Manhattan District, headed by Major General Leslie R. Groves. The primary effort, however, had come from British and American scientists working in laboratories and offices scattered throughout the nation.

Dr. J. Robert Oppenheimer, the distinguished physicist from the University of California, had set up the key establishment in the whole process at Los Alamos, New Mexico. More than any other one man, Oppenheimer is to be credited with the achievement of the completed bomb. [**418/419**]

My own knowledge of these developments had come about only after I became President, when Secretary Stimson had given me the full story. He had told me at that time that the project was nearing completion and that a bomb could be expected within another four months. It was at his suggestion, too, that I had then set up a committee of top men and had asked them to study with great care the implications the new weapon might have for us.

Secretary Stimson headed this group as chairman, and the other members were George L. Harrison, president of the New York Life Insurance Company, who was then serving as a special assistant to the Secretary of War; James F. Byrnes, as my personal representative; Ralph A. Bard, Under Secretary of the Navy; Assistant Secretary William L. Clayton for the State Department; and three of our most renowned scientists—Dr. Vannevar Bush, president of the Carnegie Institution of Washington and Director of the Office of Scientific Research and Development; Dr. Karl T. Compton, president of the Massachusetts Institute of Technology and Chief of Field Service in the Office of Scientific Research and Development; and Dr. James B. Conant, president of Harvard University and chairman of the National Defense Research Committee.

This committee was assisted by a group of scientists, of whom those most prominently connected with the development of the atomic bomb were Dr. Oppenheimer, Dr. Arthur H. Compton, Dr. E. O. Lawrence, and the Italian-born Dr. Enrico Fermi. The conclusions reached by these men, both in the advisory committee of scientists and in the larger committee, were brought to me by Secretary Stimson on June 1.

It was their recommendation that the bomb be used against the enemy as soon as it could be done. They recommended further that it should be used without specific warning and against a target that would clearly show its devastating strength. I had realized, of course, that an atomic bomb explosion would inflict damage and casualties beyond imagination. On the other hand, the scientific advisers of the committee reported, "We can propose no technical demonstration likely to bring an end to the war; we see no acceptable alternative to direct military use." It was their conclusion that no technical demonstration they might propose, such as over a deserted island, would be likely to bring the war to an end. It had to be used against an enemy target.

The final decision of where and when to use the atomic bomb was up to me. Let there be no mistake about it. I regarded the bomb as a military weapon and never had any doubt that it should be used. The top military advisers to the President recommended its use, and when I talked to Churchill he unhesitatingly told me that he favored the use of the atomic bomb if it might aid to end the war. [**419/420**]

In deciding to use this bomb I wanted to make sure that it would be used as a weapon of war in the manner prescribed by the laws of war. That meant that I wanted it dropped on a military target. I had told Stimson that the bomb should be dropped as nearly as possibly upon a war production center of prime military importance.

Stimson's staff had prepared a list of cities in Japan that might serve as targets. Kyoto, though favored by General Arnold as a center of military activity, was eliminated when Secretary Stimson pointed out that it was a cultural and religious shrine of the Japanese.

Four cities were finally recommended as targets: Hiroshima, Kokura, Niigata, and Nagasaki. They were listed in that order as targets for the first attack. The order of selection was in accordance with the military importance of these cities, but allowance would be given for weather conditions at the time of the bombing. Before the selected targets were approved as proper for military purposes, I personally went over them in detail with Stimson, Marshall, and Arnold, and we discussed the matter of timing and the final choice of the first target.

General Spaatz, who commanded the Strategic Air Forces, which would deliver the bomb on the target, was given some latitude as to when and on which of the four targets the bomb would be dropped. That was necessary because of weather and other operational considerations. In order to get preparations under way, the War Department was given orders to instruct General Spaatz that the first bomb would be dropped as soon after August 3 as weather would permit. The order to General Spaatz read as follows:

24 July 1945

TO: General Carl Spaatz
Commanding General
United States Army Strategic Air Forces

1. The 509 Composite Group, 20th Air Force will deliver its first special bomb as soon as weather will permit visual bombing after about 3 August 1945 on one of the targets: Hiroshima, Kokura, Niigata and Nagasaki. To carry military and civilian scientific personnel from the War Department to observe and record the effects of the explosion of the bomb, additional aircraft will accompany the airplane carrying the bomb. The observing planes will stay several miles distant from the point of impact of the bomb.

2. Additional bombs will be delivered on the above targets as soon as made ready by the project staff. Further instructions will be issued concerning targets other than those listed above.

3. Dissemination of any and all information concerning the use of the weapon against Japan is reserved to the Secretary of War and the President of the United States. No communique on the subject or release of information will be issued by Commanders in the field without specific prior authority. Any news stories will be sent to the War Department for special clearance. **[420/421]**

4. The foregoing directive is issued to you by direction and with the approval of the Secretary of War and the Chief of Staff, U.S.A. It is desired that you personally deliver one copy of this directive to General MacArthur and one copy to Admiral Nimitz for their information.

/s/ Thos. T. Handy
General, GSC
Acting Chief of Staff

With this order the wheels were set in motion for the first use of an atomic weapon against a military target. I had made the decision. I also instructed Stimson that the order would stand unless I notified him that the Japanese reply to our ultimatum was acceptable.

A specialized B-29 unit, known as the 509th Composite Group, had been selected for the task, and seven of the modified B-29's, with pilots and crews, were ready and waiting for orders. Meanwhile ships and planes were rushing the materials for the bomb and specialists to assemble them to the Pacific island of Tinian in the Marianas.

On July 28, Radio Tokyo announced that the Japanese government would continue to fight. There was no formal reply to the joint ultimatum of the United States, the United Kingdom, and China. There was no alternative now. The bomb was scheduled to be dropped after August 3 unless Japan surrendered before that day.

On August 6, the fourth day of the journey home from Potsdam, came the historic news that shook the world. I was eating lunch with members of the *Augusta's* crew when Captain Frank Graham, White House Map Room watch officer, handed me the following message:

TO THE PRESIDENT
FROM THE SECRETARY OF WAR

Big bomb dropped on Hiroshima August 5 at 7:15 P.M. Washington time. First reports indicate complete success which was even more conspicuous than earlier test.

. . . .

The Atomic Bomb and the Surrender of Japan*

HENRY LEWIS STIMSON (1867-1950), lawyer, diplomat, and distinguished public servant under both Democratic and Republican administrations, was the chief adviser on atomic policy to both Presidents Roosevelt and Truman. As secretary of war, Mr. Stimson had been involved in the development of the atomic bomb from the beginning, and as chairman of President Truman's Interim Committee on atomic policy, which considered the arguments for and against the bombing of Hiroshima, Mr. Stimson's role in the decision was second in importance only to the President's. Mr. Stimson's account of the circumstances surrounding use of the bomb originally appeared in *Harper's Magazine* in February, 1947 entitled "The Decision to Use the Atomic Bomb." It was subsequently reprinted in an expanded version in *On Active Service in Peace and War,* which Stimson wrote together with McGeorge Bundy.
MCGEORGE BUNDY (1919-), former professor and dean of the faculty at Harvard College, collaborated with Mr. Stimson in the preparation of his autobiography, adding important background and interpretive material to Mr. Stimson's own account. Mr. Bundy is currently associated with President Johnson's White House staff.

1. MAKING A BOMB

On August 6, 1945, an atomic bomb was dropped by an American Army airplane on the Japanese city of Hiroshima. There was thus awfully announced to the world man's mastery of a force vastly more deadly, and potentially more beneficial too, than any other in human history. In the months that followed, as Americans considered in mingled pride and fear the extraordinary achievement of the free world's scientists in combination with American engineers and industry, there was much discussion of the Hiroshima attack. As one of those largely concerned in this decision, Stimson at length concluded that it would be useful "to record for all who may be interested my understanding of the events which led up to the attack." The paper which he published in February, 1947, in *Harper's Magazine,* contains a careful record of his personal connection with this issue to which only occasional comments need be added.

"It was in the fall of 1941 that the question of atomic energy was first brought directly to my attention. At that time President Roosevelt appointed a committee consisting of Vice President Wallace, General Marshall, Dr. Vannevar Bush, Dr. James B. Conant, and myself. The function of this committee was to advise the President on questions of policy relating to the study of nuclear fission which was then proceeding both in this country and in Great Britain. For nearly four years thereafter I was directly connected with all major decisions of policy on the development and use of

* Henry L. Stimson and McGeorge Bundy, "The Atomic Bomb and the Surrender of Japan," *On Active Service in Peace and War* (New York: Harper & Brothers, 1947), pp. 612-633.

atomic energy, and from [**612/613**] May 1, 1943, until my resignation as Secretary of War on September 21, 1945, I was directly responsible to the President for the administration of the entire undertaking; my chief advisers in this period were General Marshall, Dr. Bush, Dr. Conant, and Major General Leslie R. Groves, the officer in charge of the project. At the same time I was the President's senior adviser on the military employment of atomic energy.

"The policy adopted and steadily pursued by President Roosevelt and his advisers was a simple one. It was to spare no effort in securing the earliest possible successful development of an atomic weapon. The reasons for this policy were equally simple. The original experimental achievement of atomic fission had occurred in Germany in 1938, and it was known that the Germans had continued their experiments. In 1941 and 1942 they were believed to be ahead of us, and it was vital that they should not be the first to bring atomic weapons into the field of battle. Furthermore, if we should be the first to develop the weapon, we should have a great new instrument for shortening the war and minimizing destruction. At no time, from 1941 to 1945, did I ever hear it suggested by the President, or by any other responsible member of the government, that atomic energy should not be used in the war. All of us of course understood the terrible responsibility involved in our attempt to unlock the doors to such a devastating weapon; President Roosevelt particularly spoke to me many times of his own awareness of the catastrophic potentialities of our work. But we were at war, and the work must be done. I therefore emphasize that it was our common objective, throughout the war, to be the first to produce an atomic weapon and use it. The possible atomic weapon was considered to be a new and tremendously powerful explosive, as legitimate as any other of the deadly explosive weapons of modern war. The entire purpose was the production of a military weapon; on no other ground could the wartime expenditure of so much time and money have been justified. The exact circumstances in which that weapon might be used were unknown to any of us until the middle of 1945, and when the time came, as we shall presently see, the military use of atomic energy was connected with larger questions of national policy." [**613/614**]

During these years, from 1941 to 1945, the atomic project occupied a gradually increasing proportion of Stimson's time. In addition to his duties in general supervision of the brilliant work of General Groves, he became chairman of a Combined Policy Committee, composed of British and American officials and responsible directly to the President and Prime Minister Churchill. The atomic undertaking was not solely American, although the managerial direction was exercised through American leaders working mainly with American resources. It was rather another and conspicuous example of cooperation between the United States and the British Commonwealth, in this instance represented by Great Britain and Canada, the latter being a critically important source of the necessary raw materials. In all these matters Stimson's direct agent was Bundy, who maintained constant contact with the work of General Groves and served as American secretary of the Combined Policy Committee.

A further responsibility faced by Stimson and his associates was that of securing the necessary appropriations from Congress. Until 1944 work on the atom was financed from funds elastically available from other appropriations, but as the expenditure increased, and the size of the gamble too, it was decided that direct appropriation would be necessary and that congressional leaders should be informed. Accordingly, in February, 1944, Stimson, Marshall, and Bush made their case before Speaker Rayburn and the two party leaders of the House of Representatives, Congressmen McCormack and

Martin. With great courage and co-operation these leaders piloted the necessary appropriation through the House without public discussion. A meeting in June with Senators Barkley, White, Bridges, and Thomas of Oklahoma produced similar results in the Senate. Again in 1945 further large appropriations were obtained in the same manner. Although one or two members of Congress desired to investigate the enormous construction work in Tennessee and Washington, they were successfully held off, sometimes by their own colleagues and at least once by Stimson's direct refusal to permit such investigation. Similar difficulties were surmounted in arranging for Treasury handling of atomic funds and forestalling [**614/615**] antitrust action against the Du Pont Company, whose executives must not be disturbed in their great labors for the construction of plants at Clinton and Hanford for a profit of one dollar.

"As time went on it became clear that the weapon would not be available in time for use in the European theater, and the war against Germany was successfully ended by the use of what are now called conventional means. But in the spring of 1945 it became evident that the climax of our prolonged atomic effort was at hand. By the nature of atomic chain reactions, it was impossible to state with certainty that we had succeeded until a bomb had actually exploded in a full-scale experiment; nevertheless it was considered exceedingly probable that we should by midsummer have successfully detonated the first atomic bomb. This was to be done at the Alamogordo Reservation in New Mexico. It was thus time for detailed consideration of our future plans. What had begun as a well-founded hope was now developing into a reality.

"On March 15, 1945, I had my last talk with President Roosevelt. My diary record of this conversation gives a fairly clear picture of the state of our thinking at that time. I have removed the name of the distinguished public servant who was fearful lest the Manhattan (atomic) project 'be a lemon'; it was an opinion common among those not fully informed.

" 'The President . . . had suggested that I come over to lunch today. . . . First I took up with him a memorandum which he sent to me from ——— who had been alarmed at the rumors of extravagance in the Manhattan project. ——— suggested that it might become disastrous and he suggested that we get a body of 'outside' scientists to pass upon the project because rumors are going around that Vannevar Bush and Jim Conant have sold the President a lemon on the subject and ought to be checked up on. It was rather a jittery and nervous memorandum and rather silly, and I was prepared for it and I gave the President a list of the scientists who were actually engaged on it to show the very high standing of them and it comprised four Nobel Prize men, and also how practically every physicist of standing was engaged with us in the project. Then I outlined to him the future of it and when it was likely to come off [**615/616**] and told him how important it was to get ready. I went over with him the two schools of thought that exist in respect to the future control after the war of this project, in case it is successful, one of them being the secret close-in attempted control of the project by those who control it now, and the other being the international control based upon freedom both of science and of access. I told him that those things must be settled before the first projectile is used and that he must be ready with a statement to come out to the people on it just as soon as that is done. He agreed to that. . . .'

"This conversation covered the three aspects of the question which were then uppermost in our minds. First, it was always necessary to suppress a lingering doubt that any such titanic undertaking could be successful. Second, we must consider the implications of success in terms of its long-range postwar effect. Third, we must face the problem that would be presented at the time of our first use of the weapon, for with that first use there must be some public statement."

In order to insure careful consideration of the extraordinary problems now presented, Stimson set up in April a committee "charged with the function of advising the President on the various questions raised by our apparently imminent success in developing an atomic weapon." This committee, known as the Interim Committee,[1] held discussions which "ranged over the whole field of atomic energy, in its political, military, and scientific aspects. . . . The committee's work included the drafting of the statements which were published immediately after the first bombs were dropped, the drafting of a bill for the domestic control of atomic energy, and recommendations looking toward the international control of atomic energy." [**616/617**]

But the first and greatest problem was the decision on the use of the bomb—should it be used against the Japanese, and if so, in what manner?

The Interim Committee, on June 1, recommended that the bomb should be used against Japan, without specific warning, as soon as possible, and against such a target as to make clear its devastating strength. Any other course, in the opinion of the committee, involved serious danger to the major objective of obtaining a prompt surrender from the Japanese. An advisory panel of distinguished atomic physicists reported that "We can propose no technical demonstration likely to bring an end to the war; we see no acceptable alternative to direct military use."

"The committee's function was, of course, entirely advisory. The ultimate responsibility for the recommendation to the President rested upon me, and I have no desire to veil it. The conclusions of the committee were similar to my own, although I reached mine independently. I felt that to extract a genuine surrender from the Emperor and his military advisers, there must be administered a tremendous shock which would carry convincing proof of our power to destroy the Empire. Such an effective shock would save many times the number of lives, both American and Japanese, that it would cost.

"The facts upon which my reasoning was based and steps taken to carry it out now follow." The argument which follows represents the opinion held not only by Stimson but by all his senior military advisers. General Marshall particularly was emphatic in his insistence on the shock value of the new weapon.

2. THE ACHIEVEMENT OF SURRENDER

"The principal political, social, and military objective of the United States in the summer of 1945 was the prompt and complete surrender of Japan. Only the complete destruction of her military power could open the way to lasting peace.

"Japan, in July, 1945, had been seriously weakened by our increasingly violent attacks. It was known to us that she had gone so far as to make tentative proposals to the Soviet [**617/618**] Government, hoping to use the Russians as mediators in a negotiated peace. These vague proposals contemplated the retention by Japan of important conquered areas and were therefore not considered seriously. There was as yet no indication of any weakening in the Japanese determination to fight rather than accept unconditional

[1] "I was its chairman, but the principal labor of guiding its extended deliberations fell to George L. Harrison, who acted as chairman in my absence. . . . Its members were the following, in addition to Mr. Harrison and myself:

"James F. Byrnes (then a private citizen) as personal representative of the President.

"Ralph A. Bard, Under Secretary of the Navy.

"William L. Clayton, Assistant Secretary of State.

"Dr. Vannevar Bush, Director, Office of Scientific Research and Development, and president of the Carnegie Institution of Washington.

"Dr. Karl T. Compton, Chief of the Office of Field Service in the Office of Scientific Research and Development, and president of the Massachusetts Institute of Technology.

"Dr. James B. Conant, Chairman of the National Defense Research Committee, and president of Harvard University."

surrender. If she should persist in her fight to the end, she had still a great military force.

"In the middle of July, 1945, the intelligence section of the War Department General Staff estimated Japanese military strength as follows: in the home islands, slightly under 2,000,000; in Korea, Manchuria, China proper, and Formosa, slightly over 2,000,000; in French Indo-China, Thailand, and Burma, over 200,000; in the East Indies area, including the Philippines, over 500,000; in the by-passed Pacific islands, over 100,000. The total strength of the Japanese Army was estimated at about 5,000,000 men. These estimates later proved to be in very close agreement with official Japanese figures.

"The Japanese Army was in much better condition than the Japanese Navy and Air Force. The Navy had practically ceased to exist except as a harrying force against an invasion fleet. The Air Force had been reduced mainly to reliance upon Kamikaze, or suicide, attacks. These latter, however, had already inflicted serious damage on our seagoing forces, and their possible effectiveness in a last ditch fight was a matter of real concern to our naval leaders.

"As we understood it in July, there was a very strong possibility that the Japanese Government might determine upon resistance to the end, in all the areas of the Far East under its control. In such an event the Allies would be faced with the enormous task of destroying an armed force of five million men and five thousand suicide aircraft, belonging to a race which had already amply demonstrated its ability to fight literally to the death.

"The strategic plans of our armed forces for the defeat of Japan, as they stood in July, had been prepared without reliance upon the atomic bomb, which had not yet been tested in New Mexico. We were planning an intensified sea and air blockade, and greatly intensified strategic air bombing, [**618/619**] through the summer and early fall, to be followed on November 1 by an invasion of the southern island of Kyushu. This would be followed in turn by an invasion of the main island of Honshu in the spring of 1946. The total U. S. military and naval force involved in this grand design was of the order of 5,000,000 men; if all those indirectly concerned are included, it was larger still."

(These plans did not bear any significant impress from Stimson, who was never directly concerned in the handling of Pacific strategy. In his view, however, they were wholly sound; he had been throughout 1944 and early 1945 an opponent of the contrary plan for a preliminary invasion of China, holding in the Pacific to the same general theory of the straight and heavy blow, with no diversions, which he had advocated for the European war.)

"We estimated that if we should be forced to carry this plan to its conclusion, the major fighting would not end until the latter part of 1946, at the earliest. I was informed that such operations might be expected to cost over a million casualties, to American forces alone. Additional large losses might be expected among our allies and, of course, if our campaign were successful and if we could judge by previous experience, enemy casualties would be much larger than our own.

"It was already clear in July that even before the invasion we should be able to inflict enormously severe damage on the Japanese homeland by the combined application of 'conventional' sea and air power. The critical question was whether this kind of action would induce surrender. It therefore became necessary to consider very carefully the probable state of mind of the enemy, and to assess with accuracy the line of conduct which might end his will to resist.

"With these considerations in mind, I wrote a memorandum for the President, on July 2, which I believe fairly represents the thinking of the American Government as it finally took shape in action.

This memorandum was prepared after discussion and general agreement with Joseph C. Grew, Acting Secretary of State, and Secretary of the Navy Forrestal, and when I discussed it with the President, he expressed his general approval." [**619/620**]

This memorandum was originally prompted not by the problem of atomic energy but by the American desire to achieve a Japanese surrender without invading the home islands. The distinction is an important one, and Stimson thought it worth noting that the germ of the memorandum, from which the Potsdam ultimatum later developed, was in a meeting at the White House on June 18 at which final plans for the invasion of Japan were approved. The inclusion of civilian advisers at this meeting was a return to the procedure which Franklin Roosevelt had abandoned in 1942, and the presence of Stimson and McCloy, combined with President Truman's insistent desire to be sure that there was no alternative to invasion, was the beginning of the political actions which so greatly assisted in obtaining surrender.

"July 2, 1945

"Memorandum for the President.

PROPOSED PROGRAM FOR JAPAN

"1. The plans of operation up to and including the first landing have been authorized and the preparations for the operation are now actually going on. This situation was accepted by all members of your conference on Monday, June 18.

"2. There is reason to believe that the operation for the occupation of Japan following the landing may be a very long, costly, and arduous struggle on our part. The terrain, much of which I have visited several times, has left the impression on my memory of being one which would be susceptible to a last ditch defense such as has been made on Iwo Jima and Okinawa and which of course is very much larger than either of those two areas. According to my recollection it will be much more unfavorable with regard to tank maneuvering than either the Philippines or Germany.

"3. If we once land on one of the main islands and begin a forceful occupation of Japan, we shall probably have cast the die of last ditch resistance. The Japanese are highly patriotic and certainly susceptible to calls for fanatical resistance to repel an invasion. Once started in actual invasion, we shall [**620/621**] in my opinion have to go through with an even more bitter finish fight than in Germany. We shall incur the losses incident to such a war and we shall have to leave the Japanese islands even more thoroughly destroyed than was the case with Germany. This would be due both to the difference in the Japanese and German personal character and the differences in the size and character of the terrain through which the operations will take place.

"4. A question then comes: Is there any alternative to such a forceful occupation of Japan which will secure for us the equivalent of an unconditional surrender of her forces and a permanent destruction of her power again to strike an aggressive blow at the 'peace of the Pacific'? I am inclined to think that there is enough such chance to make it well worth while our giving them a warning of what is to come and definite opportunity to capitulate. As above suggested, it should be tried before the actual forceful occupation of the homeland islands is begun and furthermore the warning should be given in ample time to permit a national reaction to set in.

"We have the following enormously favorable factors on our side—factors much weightier than those we had against Germany:

"Japan has no allies.

"Her navy is nearly destroyed and she is vulnerable to a surface and underwater blockade which can deprive her of sufficient food and supplies for her population.

"She is terribly vulnerable to our concentrated air attack upon her crowded cities, industrial and food resources.

"She has against her not only the Anglo-American forces but the rising forces of China and the ominous threat of Russia.

"We have inexhaustible and untouched industrial resources to bring to bear against her diminishing potential.

"We have great moral superiority through being the victim of her first sneak attack.

"The problem is to translate these advantages into prompt and economical achievement of our objectives. I believe Japan *is* susceptible to reason in such a crisis to a much greater extent than is indicated by our current press and other current comment. Japan is not a nation composed wholly of mad fanatics [**621/622**] of an entirely different mentality from ours. On the contrary, she has within the past century shown herself to possess extremely intelligent people, capable in an unprecedentedly short time of adopting not only the complicated technique of Occidental civilization but to a substantial extent their culture and their political and social ideas. Her advance in all these respects during the short period of sixty or seventy years has been one of the most astounding feats of national progress in history—a leap from the isolated feudalism of centuries into the position of one of six or seven great powers of the world. She has not only built up powerful armies and navies. She has maintained an honest and effective national finance and respected position in many of the sciences in which we pride ourselves. Prior to the forcible seizure of power over her government by the fanatical military group in 1931, she had for ten years lived a reasonably responsible and respectable international life.

"My own opinion is in her favor on the two points involved in this question:

"a. I think the Japanese nation has the mental intelligence and versatile capacity in such a crisis to recognize the folly of a fight to the finish and to accept the proffer of what will amount to an unconditional surrender; and

"b. I think she has within her population enough liberal leaders (although now submerged by the terrorists) to be depended upon for her reconstruction as a responsible member of the family of nations. I think she is better in this last respect than Germany was. Her liberals yielded only at the point of the pistol and, so far as I am aware, their liberal attitude has not been personally subverted in the way which was so general in Germany.

"On the other hand, I think that the attempt to exterminate her armies and her population by gunfire or other means will tend to produce a fusion of race solidity and antipathy which has no analogy in the case of Germany. We have a national interest in creating, if possible, a condition wherein the Japanese nation may live as a peaceful and useful member of the future Pacific community.

"5. It is therefore my conclusion that a carefully timed [**622/623**] warning be given to Japan by the chief representatives of the United States, Great Britain, China, and, if then a belligerent, Russia, by calling upon Japan to surrender and permit the occupation of her country in order to insure its complete demilitarization for the sake of the future peace.

"This warning should contain the following elements:

"The varied and overwhelming character of the force we are about to bring to bear on the islands.

"The inevitability and completeness of the destruction which the full application of this force will entail.

"The determination of the Allies to destroy permanently all authority and influence of those who have deceived and misled the country into embarking on world conquest.

"The determination of the Allies to limit Japanese sovereignty to her main islands and to render them powerless to mount and support another war.

"The disavowal of any attempt to extirpate the Japanese as a race or to destroy them as a nation.

"A statement of our readiness, once her economy is purged of its militaristic influence, to permit the Japanese to maintain such industries, particularly of a light consumer character, as offer no threat of aggression against their neighbors, but which can produce a sustaining economy, and provide a reasonable standard of living. The statement should indicate our willingness, for this purpose, to give Japan trade access to external raw materials, but not longer any control over the sources of supply outside her main islands. It should also indicate our willingness, in accordance with our now established foreign trade policy, in due course to enter into mutually advantageous trade relations with her.

"The withdrawal from their country as soon as the above objectives of the Allies are accomplished, and as soon as there has been established a peacefully inclined government, of a character representative of the masses of the Japanese people. I personally think that if in saying this we should add that we do not exclude a constitutional monarchy under her present dynasty, it would substantially add to the chances of acceptance.

"6. Success of course will depend on the potency of the [**623/624**] warning which we give her. She has an extremely sensitive national pride, and, as we are now seeing every day, when actually locked with the enemy will fight to the very death. For that reason the warning must be tendered before the actual invasion has occurred and while the impending destruction, though clear beyond peradventure, has not yet reduced her to fanatical despair. If Russia is a part of the threat, the Russian attack, if actual, must not have progressed too far. Our own bombing should be confined to military objectives as far as possible."

HENRY L. STIMSON
Secretary of War.

Stimson's *Harper's* account went on:

"It is important to emphasize the double character of the suggested warning. It was designed to promise destruction if Japan resisted, and hope, if she surrendered.

"It will be noted that the atomic bomb is not mentioned in this memorandum. On grounds of secrecy the bomb was never mentioned except when absolutely necessary, and furthermore, it had not yet been tested. It was of course well forward in our minds, as the memorandum was written and discussed, that the bomb would be the best possible sanction if our warning were rejected.

"The adoption of the policy outlined in the memorandum of July 2 was a decision of high politics; once it was accepted by the President, the position of the atomic bomb in our planning became quite clear. I find that I stated in my diary, as early as June 19, that 'the last chance warning . . . must be given before an actual landing of the ground forces in Japan, and fortunately the plans provide for enough time to bring in the sanctions to our warning in the shape of heavy ordinary bombing attack and an attack of S-1.' S-1 was a code name for the atomic bomb.

"There was much discussion in Washington about the timing of the warning to Japan. The controlling factor in the end was the date already set for the Potsdam meeting of the Big Three. It was President Truman's decision that such a warning should be solemnly issued by the U.S. and the U.K. from this [**624/625**] meeting, with the concurrence of the head of the Chinese Government, so that it would be plain that *all* of Japan's principal enemies were in entire unity. This was done, in the Potsdam ultimatum of July 26, which very closely followed the above memorandum of July 2, with the exception that it made no mention of the Japanese Emperor.

"On July 28 the Premier of Japan, Suzuki, rejected the Potsdam ultimatum by announcing that it was 'unworthy of public notice.' In the face of this rejection we could only proceed to demonstrate that the ultimatum had meant exactly what it said when it stated that if the Japanese continued the war, 'the full application of our military power, backed by our resolve, will mean the inevitable and complete destruction of the Japanese armed forces and just as inevitably the utter devastation of the Japanese homeland.'

"For such a purpose the atomic bomb was an eminently suitable weapon. The New Mexico test occurred while we were at Potsdam, on July 16. It was immediately clear that the power of the bomb measured up to our highest estimates. We had developed a weapon of such a revolutionary character that its use against the enemy might well be expected to produce exactly the kind of shock on the Japanese ruling oligarchy which we desired, strengthening the position of those who wished peace, and weakening that of the military party.

"Because of the importance of the atomic mission against Japan, the detailed plans were brought to me by the military staff for approval. With President Truman's warm support I struck off the list of suggested targets the city of Kyoto. Although it was a target of considerable military importance, it had been the ancient capital of Japan and was a shrine of Japanese art and culture. We determined that it should be spared. I approved four other targets including the cities of Hiroshima and Nagasaki.

"Hiroshima was bombed on August 6, and Nagasaki on August 9. These two cities were active working parts of the Japanese war effort. One was an army center; the other was naval and industrial. Hiroshima was the headquarters of the Japanese Army defending southern Japan and was a major military storage and assembly point. Nagasaki was a major [**625/626**] seaport and it contained several large industrial plants of great wartime importance. We believed that our attacks had struck cities which must certainly be important to the Japanese military leaders, both Army and Navy, and we waited for a result. We waited one day.

"Many accounts have been written about the Japanese surrender. After a prolonged Japanese Cabinet session in which the deadlock was broken by the Emperor himself, the offer to surrender was made on August 10. It was based on the Potsdam terms, with a reservation concerning the sovereignty of the Emperor."

This Japanese reservation precipitated a final discussion in Washington. For months there had been disagreement at high levels over the proper policy toward the Emperor. Some maintained that the Emperor must go, along with all the other trappings of Japanese militarism. Others urged that the war could be ended much more cheaply by openly revising the formula of "unconditional surrender" to assure the Japanese that there was no intention of removing the Emperor if it should be the desire of the Japanese people that he remain as a constitutional monarch. This latter view had been urged with particular force and skill by Joseph C. Grew, the Under Secretary of State, a man with profound insight into the Japanese character. For their pains Grew and those who agreed with him were roundly abused as appeasers.

Stimson wholly agreed with Grew's general argument, as the July 2 memorandum shows. He had hoped that a specific assurance on the Emperor might be included in the Potsdam ultimatum. Unfortunately during the war years high American officials had made some fairly blunt and unpleasant remarks about the Emperor, and it did not seem wise to Mr. Truman and Secretary of State Byrnes that the Government should reverse its field too sharply; too many people were likely to cry shame. Now, in August, the Americans were face to face with the issue they had dodged in previous months. The Japanese were ready to surrender, but, even after seeing in dreadful reality the fulfillment of Potsdam's threats, they required some assurance that the Potsdam Declaration "does [**626/627**] not comprise any demand which prejudices the prerogatives of His Majesty as a Sovereign Ruler."

August 10 was hectic in Washington.

Radio reports from Japan announced the surrender offer before official notification reached Washington by way of Switzerland. At nine o'clock Stimson was called to the White House where the President was holding a conference on the surrender terms. All those present seemed eager to make the most of this great opportunity to end the war, but there was some doubt as to the propriety of accepting the Japanese condition.

"The President then asked me what my opinion was and I told him that I thought that even if the question hadn't been raised by the Japanese we would have to continue the Emperor ourselves under our command and supervision in order to get into surrender the many scattered armies of the Japanese who would own no other authority and that something like this use of the Emperor must be made in order to save us from a score of bloody Iwo Jimas and Okinawas all over China and the New Netherlands. He was the only source of authority in Japan under the Japanese theory of the State." (Diary, August 10, 1945.)

The meeting at the White House soon adjourned to await the official surrender terms. Meanwhile Secretary Byrnes drafted a reply to which Stimson gave his prompt approval. In a later meeting this masterful paper was accepted by the President; it avoided any direct acceptance of the Japanese condition, but accomplished the desired purpose of reassuring the Japanese.

The *Harper's* article continued:

"While the Allied reply made no promises other than those already given, it implicitly recognized the Emperor's position by prescribing that his power must be subject to the orders of the Allied supreme commander. These terms were accepted on August 14 by the Japanese, and the instrument of surrender was formally signed on September 2, in Tokyo Bay. Our great objective was thus achieved, and all the evidence I have seen indicates that the controlling factor in the final Japanese decision to accept our terms of surrender was the atomic bomb."

After the *Harper's* article was published, Stimson found [**627/628**] that some of his friends retained certain doubts about the atomic decision, believing that it was based on an incorrect appreciation of the Japanese attitude. They asked whether the use of the bomb might not have been avoided if the American Government had been fully aware in the spring and early summer of the strength of the Japanese will to surrender.

This question, in Stimson's view, was based on a double misunderstanding—first, of the meaning of war, and second, of the basic purpose of the American Government during this period.

The true question, as he saw it, was not whether surrender could have been achieved without the use of the bomb but whether a different diplomatic and military course would have led to an earlier surrender. Here the question of intelligence became significant. Interviews after the war indicated clearly that a large element of the Japanese Cabinet was ready in the spring to accept substantially the same terms as those finally agreed on. Information of this general attitude was available to the American Government, but as Stimson's own paper of July 2 clearly shows, it was certainly not the view of American leaders that the Japanese already considered themselves beaten. It is possible, in the light of the final surrender, that a clearer and earlier exposition of American willingness to retain the Emperor would have produced an earlier ending to the war; this course was earnestly advocated by Grew and his immediate associates during May, 1945. But in the view of Stimson and his military advisers, it was always necessary to bear in mind that at least some of Japan's leaders would seize on any conciliatory offer as an indication of weakness. For this reason they did not support Grew in urging an immediate statement on the Emperor in May. The battle for Okinawa was proceeding slowly and with heavy losses, and they feared lest Japanese militarists argue that such a statement was the first proof of that American fatigue which they had been predicting since 1941. It seemed possible to Stimson, in 1947, that these fears had been based on a misreading of the situation.

Yet he did not believe that any intelligence reports, short of a direct report that the Japanese were fully ready to sur- [**628/629**] render, would have changed the basic American attitude. No such report was made, and none could have been made, for it was emphatically not the fact that Japan had decided on surrender before August 6; forces in the Japanese government for and against surrender continued in balance until the tenth of August. There were reports of a weakening will to resist and of "feelers" for peace terms. But such reports merely stimulated the American leaders in their desire to press home on *all* Japanese leaders the hopelessness of their cause; this was the nature of warmaking. In war, as in a boxing match, it is seldom sound for the stronger combatant to moderate his blows whenever his opponent shows signs of weakening. To Stimson, at least, the only road to early victory was to exert maximum force with maximum speed. It was not the American responsibility to throw in the sponge for the Japanese; that was one thing they must do for themselves. Only on the question of the Emperor did Stimson take, in 1945, a conciliatory view; only on this question did he later believe that history might find that the United States, by its delay in stating its position, had prolonged the war.

The second error made by critics after the war, in Stimson's view, was their assumption that American policy was, or should have been, controlled or at least influenced by a desire to avoid the use of the atomic bomb. In Stimson's view this would have been as irresponsible as the contrary course of guiding policy by a desire to insure the use of the bomb. Stimson believed, both at the time and later, that the dominant fact of 1945 was war, and that therefore, necessarily, the dominant objective was victory. If victory could be speeded by using the bomb, it should be used; if victory must be delayed in order to use the bomb, it should *not* be used. So far as he knew, this general view was fully shared by the President and all his associates. The bomb was thus not treated as a separate subject, except to determine whether it should be used at all; once that decision had been made, the timing and method of the use of the bomb were wholly subordinated to the objective of victory; no effort was made, and none was seriously considered, to achieve surrender merely in order not to have to use the bomb. Surrender was a goal sufficient in itself, wholly transcending the use or [**629/630**] nonuse of the bomb. And as it turned out, the use of the bomb, in accelerating the surrender, saved many more lives than it cost.

In concluding his *Harper's* article, Stimson considered briefly the question whether the atomic bombs had caused more damage than they prevented.

"The two atomic bombs which we had dropped were the only ones we had ready, and our rate of production at the time was very small. Had the war continued until the projected invasion on November 1, additional fire raids of B-29's would have been more destructive of life and property than the very limited number of atomic raids which we could have executed in the same period. But the atomic bomb was more than a weapon of terrible destruction; it was a psychological weapon. In March, 1945, our Air Forces had launched the first great incendiary raid on the Tokyo area. In this raid more damage was done and more casualties were inflicted than was the case at Hiroshima. Hundreds of bombers took part and hundreds of tons of incendiaries were dropped. Similar successive raids burned out a great part of the urban area of Japan, but the Japanese fought on. On August 6 one B-29 dropped a single atomic bomb on Hiroshima. Three days later a second bomb was dropped on Nagasaki and the war was over. So far as the Japanese could know, our ability to execute atomic attacks, if necessary by many planes at a time, was unlimited. As Dr. Karl Compton has said, 'it was not one atomic bomb, or two, which brought surrender; it was the experience of what an atomic bomb will actually do to a community, *plus the dread of many more,* that was effective.'[2]

"The bomb thus served exactly the purpose we intended. The peace party was able to take the path of surrender, and the whole weight of the Emperor's prestige was exerted in favor of peace. When the Emperor ordered surrender, and the small but dangerous group of fanatics who opposed him were brought under control, the Japanese became so subdued that the great undertaking of occupation and disarmament was completed with unprecedented ease." [**630/631**]

And then, in a "personal summary," Stimson reviewed the whole question as he had seen it in 1945.

"Two great nations were approaching contact in a fight to a finish which would begin on November 1, 1945. Our enemy, Japan, commanded forces of somewhat over 5,000,000 armed men. Men of these armies had already inflicted upon us, in our break-through of the outer perimeter of their defenses, over 300,000 battle casualties. Enemy armies still unbeaten had the strength to cost us a million more. *As long as the Japanese Government refused to surrender,* we should be forced to take and hold the ground, and smash the Japanese ground armies, by close-in fighting of the same desperate and costly kind that we had faced in the Pacific islands for nearly four years.

"In the light of the formidable problem which thus confronted us, I felt that every possible step should be taken to compel a surrender of the homelands, and a withdrawal of all Japanese troops from the Asiatic mainland and from other positions, before we had commenced an invasion. We held two cards to assist us in such an effort. One was the traditional veneration in which the Japanese Emperor was held by his subjects and the power which was thus vested in him over his loyal troops. It was for this reason that I suggested in my memorandum of July 2 that his dynasty should be continued. The second card was the use of the atomic bomb in the manner best calculated to persuade that Emperor and the counselors about him to submit to our demand for what was essentially unconditional surrender, placing his immense power over his people and his troops subject to our orders.

"In order to end the war in the shortest possible time and to avoid the enormous losses of human life which otherwise confronted us, I felt that we must use the Emperor as our instrument to command and compel his people to cease fighting and subject themselves to our authority through him, and that to accomplish this we must give him and his controlling advisers a compelling reason to accede to our demands. This reason furthermore must be of such a nature that his people could understand his decision. The bomb seemed to me to furnish a unique instrument for that purpose.

"My chief purpose was to end the war in victory with the [**631/632**] least possible cost in the lives of the men in the armies which I had helped to raise. In the light of the alternatives which, on a fair estimate, were open to us I believe that no man, in our position and subject to our responsibilities, holding in his hands a weapon of such possibilities for accomplishing this purpose and saving those lives, could have failed to use it and afterwards looked his countrymen in the face."

He might have added here a still more personal comment. In March he visited an Air Forces redistribution center in Florida. There he met and talked with men on their way to the Pacific after completing a term of duty in Europe. The impression he received was profound. These men were weary in a way that no one merely reading reports could readily

[2] K. T. Compton, "The Atomic Bomb and the Surrender of Japan," *Atlantic Monthly,* January, 1947.

understand. They would go to the Pacific, and they would fight well again, but after this meeting Stimson realized more clearly than ever that the primary obligation of any man responsible for and to these Americans was to end the war as quickly as possible. To discard or fail to use effectively any weapon that might spare them further sacrifice would be irresponsibility so flagrant as to deserve condign punishment. Paraphrasing Shakespeare (but with life and not death as his end), Stimson could have said, as he felt, that "He hates them who would upon the rack of this tough war stretch them out longer."

And yet to use the atomic bomb against cities populated mainly by civilians was to assume another and scarcely less terrible responsibility. For thirty years Stimson had been a champion of international law and morality. As soldier and Cabinet officer he had repeatedly argued that war itself must be restrained within the bounds of humanity. As recently as June 1 he had sternly questioned his Air Forces leader, wanting to know whether the apparently indiscriminate bombings of Tokyo were absolutely necessary. Perhaps, as he later said, he was misled by the constant talk of "precision bombing," but he had believed that even air power could be limited in its use by the old concept of "legitimate military targets." Now in the conflagration bombings by massed B-29's he was permitting a kind of total war he had always hated, and in recommending the use of the atomic bomb he was implicitly confessing that there could be no significant limits to the horror of [**632/633**] modern war. The decision was not difficult, in 1945, for peace with victory was a prize that outweighed the payment demanded. But Stimson could not dodge the meaning of his action. The following were the last two paragraphs of his article:

"As I read over what I have written, I am aware that much of it, in this year of peace, may have a harsh and unfeeling sound. It would perhaps be possible to say the same things and say them more gently. But I do not think it would be wise. As I look back over the five years of my service as Secretary of War, I see too many stern and heart-rending decisions to be willing to pretend that war is anything else than what it is. The face of war is the face of death; death is an inevitable part of every order that a wartime leader gives. The decision to use the atomic bomb was a decision that brought death to over a hundred thousand Japanese. No explanation can change that fact and I do not wish to gloss it over. But this deliberate, premeditated destruction was our least abhorrent choice. The destruction of Hiroshima and Nagasaki put an end to the Japanese war. It stopped the fire raids, and the strangling blockade; it ended the ghastly specter of a clash of great land armies.

"In this last great action of the Second World War we were given final proof that war is death. War in the twentieth century has grown steadily more barbarous, more destructive, more debased in all its aspects. Now, with the release of atomic energy, man's ability to destroy himself is very nearly complete. The bombs dropped on Hiroshima and Nagasaki ended a war. They also made it wholly clear that we must never have another war. This is the lesson men and leaders everywhere must learn, and I believe that when they learn it they will find a way to lasting peace. There is no other choice."

Control of Atomic Energy*

JAMES FRANCIS BYRNES (1879-) has occupied a wide variety of important national and state offices, including member of Congress, United States senator, justice of the Supreme Court, director of economic stabilization, director of war mobilization, secretary of state, and governor of South Carolina. Mr. Byrnes was President Truman's special representative on the Interim Committee which discussed and recommended use of the atomic bomb.

I do not remember just when it was that President Roosevelt told me about the atomic bomb. I do remember that it was a hot summer afternoon and the two of us were sitting alone in his oval office discussing certain phases of the war mobilization program. Suddenly, and for no apparent reason, he began to tell me the awesome story of the Manhattan Project.

I confess I thought the story fantastic. I was sure the President was exaggerating the possibilities just to watch my amazed reaction. I didn't disappoint him. And, as he noted my amazement, he proceeded with obvious pleasure to astound me with the scientists' prediction of what atomic energy would do. He told me that, prior to 1939, the Germans had made some progress with their experiments and he knew they were continuing their efforts. It was a race between us, he said, to see who could develop the first bomb.

At that time, which I believe was the summer of 1943, the President thought the Germans were ahead of us in the atomic race. It was evident that the information on which he based his belief contained more speculation than fact. Our Intelligence agents necessarily were restricted in securing accurate information on such a highly technical matter. From what we learned after the war, it was clear that the President had overestimated the progress of the Germans in this respect. Nevertheless, such reports served to stimulate the extraordinary efforts put forth on the Manhattan Project.

After the first discussion, neither the President nor I mentioned the atomic project to each other for many months. In fact, no one ever talked about it unless it was absolutely necessary. I remember once mentioning it to Secretary of War Stimson who, from its very inception, personally supervised the Manhattan Project. His reaction indicated surprise that I knew about it.

Even if the President had not told me about the project, as Director of War Mobilization I could not have avoided noting certain aspects of an enterprise as colossal as this. It, of course, held a top priority both for men and materiel. With manpower one of our most critical shortages, a [**257/258**] project that at its peak claimed the labor of 125,000 men could not escape my notice, particularly since so many of the workers were highly skilled technicians.

However, I was not directly concerned with the project and was too busy to be curious. Thus it was not until December

* James F. Byrnes, from "Control of Atomic Energy," *Speaking Frankly* (New York: Harper & Brothers, 1947), pp. 257-265.

1944, when another aspect of the labor situation brought me into the picture, that I learned definitely of the great progress we had been making.

An effort was being made to organize the workers at the Oak Ridge plant; controversies over the jurisdiction of the labor organizations involved had arisen and these had been referred to the National Labor Relations Board. The public hearing required under the circumstances had been postponed four times at the War Department's request; no further postponement was possible.

Under Secretary of War Robert Patterson and Major General Leslie R. Groves came over to the White House to discuss the problem with me. General Groves pointed out that the hearing would require the presentation of evidence on such things as the number of workers employed, the number to be employed, the relationship of a particular unit to the project as a whole, and so on. Such evidence, General Groves was convinced, would necessitate disclosures that would seriously jeopardize the security of the project. They thought it would be helpful if I would arrange a meeting at the White House for the three of us and the leaders of the labor organizations involved. I agreed.

During our discussions, Mr. Patterson said that the War Department would know by April 1, 1945, whether or not they could develop the bomb. Both he and General Groves thought the effort would succeed, and they were confident they would know one way or the other by that date. It was the first time I had heard anyone venture to name a date.

The conference was arranged for the morning of December 5. The union officials were Mr. Joseph P. Clark of the International Brotherhood of Firemen and Oilers and Mr. Al Wegener of the International Brotherhood of Electrical Workers.

We took these men into our confidence. We told them that few people knew about the project. At that time, I believe, only four members of Congress had been given any concrete information. We asked the labor officials to waive their rights under the Wagner Act and to co-operate with General Groves in protecting the security of the project. They were good and patriotic men. They agreed to help and left immediately to do so. They were given authority to explain the situation to the presidents of their respective unions, Mr. John F. McNamara and Mr. Edward J. Brown; both of these leaders likewise promised their full co-operation. Their promise involved sacrificing rights given them by the law, but they kept **[258/259]** it. They convinced the local union leaders, and the secret was protected for the duration of the war.

As a matter of fact, it was always amazing to me that the project did not become more generally known. It also was surprising that the Congress was willing to appropriate approximately two billion dollars without demanding more information on the use to which it was being put. It is a great tribute to those few congressional leaders who did have some idea of the nature of the project that they resisted the temptation to tell their colleagues and thus share the great responsibility.

The April 1 deadline came, but the result of the gigantic effort still was in doubt. Secretary Stimson, however, was confident of success. He instilled his confidence in the President. I am glad he did. But I have always regretted that President Roosevelt died without knowing definitely that the project was a success: It had been undertaken and carried to a conclusion solely because of his vision and courage in the days when the effort seemed hopeless.

Shortly after President Roosevelt's death, Secretary Stimson told President Truman that the scientists and others who had been working under his direction felt confident they would produce an atomic bomb within a very short time. He suggested the appointment of an Interim Committee to consider and make recommendations to the President on such important questions of policy as the test of the bomb, its use in the war, and the postwar use of atomic energy. [**259/260**]

. . . .

In the first meeting of the Interim Committee, Doctors Bush, Conant and Compton described the destructive power of the bomb. After hearing them, I was confident that, when developed, it would bring a speedy end to the war in the Pacific. I remembered that as a member of the Senate committee handling naval appropriations I had often heard naval officers say that a new defensive weapon was developed for every offensive weapon. I asked the scientists what defense there could be against the atomic bomb. But these distinguished gentlemen, who had directed the advisory work on the bomb, could think of no defense. They did anticipate the development of still larger and more destructive bombs. I asked them if I should believe the only defense against further development was to kill off all the scientists. This suggestion did not appeal to them.

After listening to the scientists discuss the development of the project, we spent a day with the industrialists and engineers who had performed the amazing task of constructing the huge plants in Tennessee and Wash- [**260/261**] ington and of installing the manufacturing processes that produced the bomb. Because it was a vital point in any decision on a system of control, I asked both groups how long it might take other governments to produce atomic bombs. The question, of course, was not only one of physics, but one of materials, of engineering skills, of technical know-how, and many other factors. From all the information we received, I concluded that any other government would need from seven to ten years, at least, to produce a bomb. And I think that to accomplish the task at such speed would require a quicker return to normal conditions than has taken place in any country within the last few years.

On July 1, 1945, the Interim Committee unanimously recommended to the Presi dent that the bomb be used against Japan as soon as possible. It added that the bomb should be used only where war plants or military installations were located. With the exception of Mr. Bard, the committee recommended that it be used without warning. This last question we had carefully considered.

We feared that, if the Japanese were told that the bomb would be used on a given locality, they might bring our boys who were prisoners of war to that area. Also, the experts had warned us that the static test which was to take place in New Mexico, even if successful, would not be conclusive proof that a bomb would explode when dropped from an airplane. If we were to warn the Japanese of the new highly destructive weapon in the hope of impressing them and if the bomb then failed to explode, certainly we would have given aid and comfort to the Japanese militarists. Thereafter, the Japanese people probably would not be impressed by any statement we might make in the hope of inducing them to surrender.

Arrangements for the test in New Mexico also were a problem for the committee. Because no one could be sure what the full results of the first atomic explosion might be, arrangements had to be made to evacuate the whole area if necessary. We knew that under the best circumstances the explosion would reverberate so far that secrecy would be difficult to maintain. News releases, with stories to meet every foreseeable contingency, were prepared and were to be issued to the publice only if the circumstances required.

As the President's representative on the committee, it was my duty to report to him the reasons for our various recommendations. Throughout our deliberations, I told him, we relied on the estimates of the military situation presented by the Joint Chiefs of Staff. Their plans called for an invasion of Kyushu, the southernmost island of the Japanese homeland, on November 1. This was to be followed by an invasion of the main island of Honshu in the spring of 1946.

The Joint Chiefs anticipated that more than five million of our armed forces would be engaged. The Japanese armies were then estimated at about five million —an estimate we later [**261/262**] found was quite accurate. Secretary Forrestal had told me that the Japanese air force suicide attacks were increasing our losses in ships and in human lives. These attacks gained in intensity the closer we got to Japan; it was certain that an invasion force would be attacked with far greater fury and recklessness. The military experts informed us that, from the facts at their disposal, they believed our invasion would cost us a million casualties, to say nothing of those of our Allies and of the enemy.

I reported these conclusions to the President. I also told him what the scientists, engineers and industrialists, who had come before the committee, had to say. He expressed the opinion that, regrettable as it might be, so far as he could see, the only reasonable conclusion was to use the bomb.

While we were aboard the *Augusta* en route to Potsdam, the final preparations were under way in New Mexico for the crucial test. The day the greatest blast the world had yet known was reverberating over the sands of Alamagordo, the President, Admiral Leahy and I were looking at the rubble that had been Berlin. Reports of the test, which had to be transmitted in top secret codes, did not reach us for several days. By that time, the conference was in full swing; I was so busy that I have never been able to recall the time and circumstances under which Secretary Stimson brought us the news. Another reason the moment made so little impression on me was that my work on the Interim Committee had already convinced me that the bomb would succeed. News of the test seemed simply a confirmation of a well-known fact.

Prime Minister Churchill, whose cooperation with President Roosevelt had contributed so much to the success of the great gamble, was intensely interested in the reports. He discussed the project at length with President Truman and was eager to hear from me about the work of the Interim Committee. In addition to his tremendous interest in the effect of the bomb on the war with Japan, he foresaw more clearly than many others the possibilities presented by the release of atomic energy.

We faced a terrible decision. We could not rely on Japan's inquiries to the Soviet Union about a negotiated peace as proof that Japan would surrender unconditionally without the use of the bomb. In fact, Stalin stated the last message to him had said that Japan would "fight to the death rather than accept unconditional surrender." Under those circumstances, agreement to negotiate could only arouse false hopes. Instead, we relied upon the Potsdam Declaration.

As soon as we had studied all the reports from New Mexico, the President and I concluded we should tell Generalissimo Stalin that we had developed the bomb and proposed to use it unless Japan acceded promptly to our demand for surrender. The Soviet Government was not at war with [**262/263**] Japan, but we had been informed of their intention to enter the war and felt, therefore, that Stalin should know.

At the close of the meeting of the Big Three on the afternoon of July 24, the President walked around the large circular table to talk to Stalin. After a brief conversation the President rejoined me and we rode back to the "Little White House" together. He said he had told Stalin that, after long experimentation, we had developed a new bomb far more destructive than any other known bomb, and that we planned to use it very soon unless Japan surrendered. Stalin's only reply was to say that he was glad to hear of the bomb and he hoped we would use it. I was surprised at Stalin's lack of interest. I concluded that he had not grasped the importance of the discovery. I thought that the following day he would ask for more information about it. He did not. Later I concluded that, because the Russians kept secret their developments in military weapons, they thought it improper to ask us about ours.

Two nights after the talk with Stalin, the Potsdam Declaration was issued. We devoutly hoped that the Japanese would heed our warning that, unless they surrendered unconditionally, the destruction of their armed forces and the devastation of their homeland was inevitable. But, on July 28, the Japanese Premier issued a statement saying the declaration was unworthy of notice. That was disheartening. There was nothing left to do but use the bomb. Secretary Stimson had selected targets of military importance and President Truman approved his plans. Shortly thereafter Secretary Stimson left for the United States.

Despite the Japanese Premier's statement, I continued to hope the Japanese Government would change its mind. I was greatly disappointed when August 2, the day of our departure from Potsdam, arrived and no further word had been received. I recognized then that our hope of avoiding use of the bomb was virtually gone. [**263/264**]

. . . .

I thought that the bombing of Hiroshima, southern headquarters and depot for the homeland army, would convince the Japanese that the Allied nations meant what they said in the Potsdam Declaration. Millions of leaflets were dropped warning the Japanese that one out of ten listed cities would be the next target. We received no communication from them and so, on August 8, the second bomb was dropped on Nagasaki, a major seaport with many war plants.

As at Hiroshima, the destruction in Nagasaki was terrific. The Emperor did not wait for further evidence of our intention to carry out the Potsdam Declaration. He broke the deadlock that had existed for several days in the Japanese Cabinet; on August 10, he submitted the offer of surrender. No one should doubt that the destruction wrought by the atomic bomb influenced the action of the Emperor and the Cabinet.

Those two bombs were all we then had ready for use, but others were on the way and some were expected to be even more powerful. In these two raids there were many casualties but not nearly so many as there would have been had our air force continued to drop incendiary bombs on Japan's cities. Certainly, by bringing the war to an end, the atomic bomb saved the lives of thousands of American boys. [**264/265**]

No one who played a part in the development of the bomb or in our decision to use it felt happy about it. It was natural and right that men should worry about performing a duty that would cost so many human lives. Most of these men were civilians, but I have no doubt that all thinking men in the armed forces felt the same way about air raids, the dropping of incendiary bombs and similar actions which cost many lives. Being soldiers, they did not write to the press about their views as did the civilians. But the truth is, war remains what General Sherman said it was.

. . . .

Atom Bombs, Germs—and Peace*

WILLIAM DANIEL LEAHY (1875-1959) rose to the rank of admiral and chief of naval operations before the outbreak of World War II. During the war he was recalled from retirement by President Roosevelt to serve in a number of diplomatic assignments. In 1942 he became President Roosevelt's chief of staff, and he continued to serve President Truman in an advisory capacity. Among the high-ranking military officers who were consulted concerning the use of atomic bombs, Admiral Leahy was the most vigorous in his opposition.

. . . .

A few months after I took over as Chief of Staff to the President I became acquainted in general with the status of both of these projects [the development of the atomic bomb and of instruments of bacteriological warfare]. In November, 1942, . . . I discussed with President George Merck, of the well-known chemical firm bearing his name, the possible use of bacteriological warfare. Merck was then studying, with a considerable number of scientists, and in high secrecy, both offensive employment of, and preventive measures against, germ warfare.

At intervals this subject came up in my conversations with President Roosevelt and later with President Truman. I recall particularly that, as we were sailing for Honolulu for the MacArthur-Nimitz conferences in July of 1944, there was a spirited discussion of bacteriological war- [**439/440**] fare in the President's cabin. By that time the scientists thought, for example, that they could destroy completely the rice crop of Japan. Some of those present advocated the adoption of such measures.

Personally, I recoiled from the idea and said to Roosevelt, "Mr. President, this (using germs and poison) would violate every Christian ethic I have ever heard of and all of the known laws of war. It would be an attack on the noncombatant population of the enemy. The reaction can be foretold—if we use it, the enemy will use it." Roosevelt remained noncommittal throughout this discussion, but the United States did not resort to bacteriological warfare.

. . . .

Both sides were prepared throughout the war that had just ended to unloose deadly gases, but not even the fanatical followers of Hitler and Hirohito, who committed so many other unspeakable atrocities, dared use poison gas—for fear of retaliation.

To me, the atomic bomb belongs in exactly the same category.

I have admitted frankly in the preceding chapter that I misjudged the terrible efficiency of this entirely new concept of an explosive. In the fall of 1944 I held conferences with Professor Bush, Lord Cherwell, the British expert on atomic energy, and Major General Groves. They had convinced President Roosevelt and Prime Minister Churchill of the potential effectiveness of atomic energy for military purposes. As a [**440/441**] result, vast sums of money were appropriated to push the development with all possible speed.

In the spring of 1945 President Truman directed Mr. Byrnes to make a special study of the status and prospects of the

* William D. Leahy, from "Atom Bombs, Germs—and Peace," *I Was There* (New York: Whittlesey House-McGraw-Hill Book Co., Inc., 1950), pp. 439-442.

new atomic explosive on which two billion dollars already had been spent. Byrnes came to my home on the evening of June 4 to discuss his findings. He was more favorably impressed than I had been up to that time with the prospects of success in the final development and use of this new weapon.

Once it had been tested, President Truman faced the decision as to whether to use it. He did not like the idea, but was persuaded that it would shorten the war against Japan and save American lives. It is my opinion that the use of this barbarous weapon at Hiroshima and Nagasaki was of no material assistance in our war against Japan. The Japanese were already defeated and ready to surrender because of the effective sea blockade and the successful bombing with conventional weapons.

It was my reaction that the scientists and others wanted to make this test because of the vast sums that had been spent on the project. Truman knew that, and so did the other people involved. However, the Chief Executive made a decision to use the bomb on two cities in Japan. We had only produced two bombs at that time. We did not know which cities would be the targets, but the President specified that the bombs should be used against military facilities.

I realized that my original error in discounting the effectiveness of the atomic bomb was based on long experience with explosives in the Navy. I had specialized in gunnery and at one time headed the Navy Department's Bureau of Ordnance. "Bomb" is the wrong word to use for this new weapon. It is not a bomb. It is not an explosive. It is a poisonous thing that kills people by its deadly radioactive reaction, more than by the explosive force it develops.

The lethal possibilities of atomic warfare in the future are frightening. My own feeling was that in being the first to use it, we had adopted an ethical standard common to the barbarians of the Dark Ages. I was not taught to make war in that fashion, and wars cannot be won by destroying women and children. We were the first to have this weapon in our possession, and the first to use it. There is a practical certainty that potential enemies will have it in the future and that atomic bombs will sometime be used against us.

That is why, as a professional military man with a half century of service to his government, I come to the end of my war story with an apprehension about the future.

These new concepts of "total war" are basically distasteful to the soldier and sailor of my generation. Employment of the atomic bomb [**441/442**] in war will take us back in cruelty toward noncombatants to the days of Genghis Khan.

It will be a form of pillage and rape of a society, done impersonally by one state against another, whereas in the Dark Ages it was a result of individual greed and vandalism. These new and terrible instruments of uncivilized warfare represent a modern type of barbarism not worthy of Christian man.

One of the professors associated with the Manhattan Project told me that he had hoped the bomb wouldn't work. I wish that he had been right.

Perhaps there is some hope that its capacity for death and terror among the defenseless may restrain nations from using the atom bomb against each other, just as in the last war such fears made them avoid employment of the new and deadlier poison gases developed since World War I.

However, I am forced to a reluctant conclusion that for the security of my own country which has been the guiding principle in my approach to all problems faced during my career, there is but one course open to us:

Until the United Nations, or some world organization, can guarantee—and have the power to enforce that guarantee—that the world will be spared the terrors of atomic warfare, the United States must have more and better atom bombs than any potential enemy.

The Emperor of Japan and Japan's Surrender*

JOSEPH CLARK GREW (1880-) has occupied a number of high diplomatic positions, including ambassador to Japan (1931-1941), director of the Office of Far Eastern Affairs in the Department of State (1944), under-secretary of state (1944-1945), and acting-secretary of state (1945). As one of the country's leading experts on Japan, Mr. Grew believed the Japanese could be persuaded to surrender if the safety of their Emperor were guaranteed, and he attempted to have such a guarantee included in the Potsdam Declaration, the Allied ultimatum delivered to Japan before the bombing of Hiroshima. The text of the Potsdam Declaration is included in the selection from Shigenori Togo's *The Cause of Japan*, reprinted on page 72.

. . . .

JAPAN'S SURRENDER[6]

Much light has been shed since the war, in books, articles and reports from Americans in Japan during the occupation, on the developments leading up to Japan's surrender in August, 1945.[7] For a long time I had held the belief, based on my intimate experience with Japanese thinking and psychology over an extensive period, that the surrender of the Japanese would be highly unlikely, regardless of military defeat, in the absence of a public undertaking by the President that unconditional surrender would not mean the elimination of the present dynasty if the Japanese people desired its retention. I furthermore believed that if such a statement could be formulated and issued shortly after the great devastation of Tokyo by our B-29 attacks on or about May 26, 1945, the hands of the Emperor and his peace-minded advisers would be greatly [**1421/1422**] strengthened in the face of the intransigent militarists and that the process leading to an early surrender might even then be set in motion by such a statement. Soviet Russia had not then entered the war against Japan, and since the United States had carried the major burden of the war in the Pacific, and since the President had already publicly declared that unconditional surrender would mean neither annihilation nor enslavement, I felt that the President would be fully justified in amplifying his previous statement as suggested.[8] My belief in the potential effect of such a statement at that particular juncture was fully shared and supported by those officers in the Department of State who knew Japan and the Japanese well, especially by Eu-

[6] Mr. Grew wrote this statement in 1950.

[7] See especially Toshikazu Kase, *Journey to the Missouri.*

[8] In a statement issued to the press on May 8, 1945, President Truman had said: "Our blows will not cease until the Japanese military and naval forces lay down their arms in *unconditional surrender.*

"Just what does the unconditional surrender of the armed forces mean for the Japanese people?

"It means the end of the war.

"It means the termination of the influence of the military leaders who have brought Japan to the present brink of disaster.

"It means provision for the return of soldiers and sailors to their families, their farms, their jobs.

"It means not prolonging the present agony and suffering of the Japanese in the vain hope of victory.

"Unconditional surrender does not mean the extermination or enslavement of the Japanese people." U.S. Department of State, *The Department of State Bulletin,* May 13, 1945, p. 886.

* Joseph C. Grew, from "The Emperor of Japan and Japan's Surrender," *Turbulent Era,* ed. Walter Johnson, 2 vols. (Boston: Houghton Mifflin Co., 1952), II, 1421-1428. Reprinted with the permission of the publishers.

gene H. Dooman [*sic*], formerly Counselor of the American Embassy in Tokyo, Joseph W. Ballantine, Director of the Office of Far Eastern Affairs in the State Department, Professor George Hubbard Blakeslee, Chairman of the Far Eastern Area Committee of the State Department, all of whom I regarded as among our soundest experts on Japanese affairs, and others.[9] [**1422/1423**]

Then, on my own initiative, as Acting Secretary of State, I called on President Truman on May 28, 1945, and presented this thesis as set forth in a memorandum prepared immediately after that meeting, a copy of which I read aloud at a further conference in the Pentagon Building on May 29, 1945, in the presence of the Secretaries of War and Navy and the Chiefs of Staff. I also handed the President on May 28 a draft of a proposed statement which we in the State Department had prepared after long and most careful consideration.

In my own talk with the President on May 28, he immediately said that his own thinking ran along the same lines as mine, but he asked me to discuss the proposal with the Secretaries of War and Navy and the Chiefs of Staff and then to report to him the consensus of that group.[10] A conference was [**1423/1424**] therefore called and was held in the office of the Secretary of War in the Pentagon Building on May 29, 1945, and the issue was discussed for an hour. According to my memorandum of that meeting it became clear in the course of the discussion that Mr. Stimson, Mr. Forrestal, and General Marshall (Admiral King was absent) were all in accord with the principle of the proposal but that for certain military reasons, not then divulged, it was considered inadvisable for the President to make such a statement at that juncture. It later appeared that the fighting on Okinawa was still going on, and it was felt that such a declaration as I proposed would be interpreted by the Japanese as a confession of weakness. The question of timing was the nub of the whole matter, according to the views expressed. I duly reported this to the President, and the proposal for action was, for the time being, dropped.

When Mr. Byrnes became Secretary of State over a month later, I endeavored to interest him in the importance and ur-

[9] Dr. Alexander H. Leighton in his book, *Human Relations in a Changing World* (New York: E. P. Dutton & Co., 1949), p. 55, wrote that "during the winter and spring of 1945 the analysts [of the OWI] Foreign Morale Analysis Division of the OWI] strongly advised the policy makers against employing attacks on the Emperor or the imperial institution in psychological warfare. It was believed that such lines would at best be wasteful and could well harden enemy resistance. On the other hand, the analysts thought that the Emperor might be turned to good use in lowering resistance if the enemy were told that the decision regarding his fate after an Allied victory would be up to the Japanese themselves." Leighton also stated, p. 126, that it "is evident from what has been presented here that as early as May, 1945, the Division had concluded that the Japanese determination to fight was seriously undermined. . . . The first indicators of the downward trend had been noted as early as January."

In *Great Mistakes of the War* (New York: Harper & Bros., 1950), pp. 92, 95, Hanson Baldwin wrote: "It is therefore clear today—and was clear to many even as early as the spring of 1945—that the military defeat of Japan was certain." The United States "demanded unconditional surrender, then dropped the bomb and accepted conditional surrender, a sequence which indicates pretty clearly that the Japanese would have surrendered, even if the bomb had not been dropped, had the Potsdam Declaration included our promise to permit the Emperor to remain on his imperial throne."

"More important, however," wrote Admiral Ellis M. Zacharias in *Secret Missions* (New York: G. P. Putnam's Sons, 1946), p. 335, "were recent intelligence reports disclosing a definite Japanese trend which could be exploited to move the Japanese toward surrender, or at least a termination of hostilities prior to our invasion of Japan proper. Among these was a very significant report given in the utmost secrecy to one of our intelligence officers in a neutral capital. It outlined in great detail the course Japan intended to take and stated that General Koiso would soon resign and permit the appointment as prime minister of Admiral Suzuki, an old confidant of the Emperor and leader of what I even then had come to call the 'peace party.' Moreover, the document indicated that the Emperor himself was leading a group of influential personalities desirous of obtaining peace terms under the most favorable circumstances."

[10] James Forrestal on page 69 of the book *The Forrestal Diaries* (New York: The Viking Press, 1951), edited by Walter Millis with the collaboration of E. S. Duffield, says, "Mr. Grew was of the impression that the President had indicated that he was not in accord with this point of view" (that we should indicate now that the Japanese, after surrender, should be allowed to retain their own form of government). Mr. Forrestal was clearly mistaken in this conception of what I had said. I made it quite clear in the meeting in Secretary Stimson's office on May 29, 1945, attended by numerous witnesses, that on this point the President had assured me that "his own thinking ran along the same lines as mine" but that he wished me to consult our military and naval authorities.—J. C. G.

gency of a public statement along the lines proposed, but during those few days he was intensely occupied in preparing for the Potsdam Conference, and it was only on the morning of his departure for Potsdam that I was able to hand him a draft on which a declaration might be based. This was the draft I had shown to the President. Mr. Byrnes was already on his way out of his office to drive to the airport, and his last action before leaving was to place our draft in his pocket. Mr. Stimson was then already in Europe and I urged Jack McCloy, Assistant Secretary of War, when he met him over there, to tell Mr. Stimson how strongly I felt about the matter.

Mr. Stimson did take energetic steps at Potsdam to secure the decision by the President and Mr. Churchill to issue the [**1424/1425**] proclamation. In fact, the opinion was expressed to me by one American already in Potsdam, that if it had not been for Mr. Stimson's wholehearted initiative, the Potsdam Conference would have ended without any proclamation to Japan being issued at all. But even Mr. Stimson was unable to have included in the proclamation a categorical undertaking that unconditional surrender would not mean the elimination of the dynasty if the Japanese people desired its retention.

The main point at issue historically is whether, if immediately following the terrific devastation of Tokyo by our B-29s in May, 1945,[11] "the President had made a public categorical statement that surrender would not mean the elimination of the present dynasty if the Japanese people desired its retention, the surrender of Japan could have been hastened.

"That question can probably never be definitively answered but a good deal of evidence is available to shed light on it. From statements made by a number of the moderate former Japanese leaders to responsible Americans after the American occupation, it is quite clear that the civilian advisers to the Emperor were working toward surrender long before the Potsdam Proclamation, even indeed before my talk with the President on May 28, for they knew then that Japan was a defeated nation. The stumbling block that they had to overcome was the complete dominance of the Japanese Army over the Government, and even when the moderates finally succeeded in getting a decision by the controlling element of the Government to accept the Potsdam terms, efforts were made by the unreconciled elements in the Japanese Army to bring about nullification of that decision. The Emperor needed all the support he could get, and in the light of available evidence I myself and others felt and still feel that if such a categorical statement about the dynasty had been issued in May, 1945, the surrender-minded elements in the Government might well have been afforded by such a statement a valid reason and the necessary strength to come to an early clear-cut decision.

"If surrender could have been brought about in May, 1945, or [**1425/1426**] even in June or July, before the entrance of Soviet Russia into the war and the use of the atomic bomb, the world would have been the gainer.

"The action of Prime Minister Suzuki in rejecting the Potsdam ultimatum by announcing on July 28, 1945, that it was 'unworthy of public notice' was a most unfortunate if not an utterly stupid step. Suzuki, who was severely wounded and very nearly assassinated as a moderate by the military extremists in 1936, I believe from the evidence which has reached me was surrender-minded even before May, 1945, if only it were made clear that surrender would not involve the downfall of the dynasty. That point was clearly *implied* in Article 12 of the Potsdam Proclamation that 'The occupying forces of the Allies shall be withdrawn from Japan as soon as . . . there has been established in accordance with the freely expressed will of the Japanese people a peacefully inclined and responsible government.'

[11] The following quotation is taken from a letter to Mr. Henry L. Stimson, February 12, 1947.

This however was not, at least from the Japanese point of view, a categorical undertaking regarding the dynasty, nor did it comply with your [Henry L. Stimson's] suggestion that it would substantially add to the chances of acceptance if the ultimatum should contain a statement that we would not exclude a constitutional monarchy under the present dynasty.[12]

[12] See Henry L. Stimson and McGeorge Bundy, *On Active Service in Peace and War* (New York: Harper & Bros., 1948), pp. 619-27, where Mr. Stimson has written: "I wrote a memorandum for the President, on July 2, which I believe fairly represents the thinking of the American Government as it finally took shape in action. This memorandum was prepared after discussion and general agreement with Joseph C. Grew, Acting Secretary of State, and Secretary of the Navy Forrestal, and when I discussed it with the President, he expressed his general approval." In this memorandum Mr. Stimson said that he felt that a statement should be issued to the Japanese, assuring them among other things of the "withdrawal from their country as soon as the above objectives of the Allies are accomplished, and as soon as there has been established a peacefully inclined government, of a character representative of the masses of the Japanese people. I personally think that if in saying this we should add that we do not exclude a constitutional monarchy under her present dynasty, it would substantially add to the chances of acceptance."

In an article in the February, 1947, issue of *Harper's Magazine* Mr. Stimson further explained his position in 1945. *On Active Service* contains quotations from this *Harper's* article with Stimson's and Bundy's further comments and explanations.

" 'Many accounts have been written about the Japanese surrender. After a prolonged Japanese Cabinet session in which the deadlock was broken by the Emperor himself, the offer to surrender was made on August 10. It was based on the Potsdam terms, with a reservation concerning the sovereignty of the Emperor.'

"This Japanese reservation precipitated a final discussion in Washington. For months there had been disagreement at high levels over the proper policy toward the Emperor. Some maintained that the Emperor must go, along with all the other trappings of Japanese militarism. Others urged that the war could be ended much more cheaply by openly revising the formula of 'unconditional surrender' to assure the Japanese that there was no intention of removing the Emperor if it should be the desire of the Japanese people that he remain as a constitutional monarch. This latter view had been urged with particular force and skill by Joseph C. Grew, the Under Secretary of State, a man with profound insight into the Japanese character. For their pains Grew and those who agreed with him were roundly abused as appeasers.

"Stimson wholly agreed with Grew's general argument, as the July 2 memorandum shows. He had hoped that a specific assurance on the Emperor might be included in the Potsdam ultimatum. Unfortunately during the war years high American officials had made some fairly blunt and unpleasant remarks about the Emperor, and it did not seem wise to Mr. Truman and Secretary of State Brynes that the Government should reverse its field too sharply; too many people were likely to cry shame. Now, in August, the Americans were face to face with the issue they had dodged in previous months. The Japanese were ready to surrender, but, even after seeing in dreadful reality the fulfillment of Potsdam's threats, they required some assurance that the Potsdam Declaration 'does not comprise any demand which prejudices the prerogatives of His Majesty as a Sovereign Ruler.'

"August 10 was hectic in Washington. Radio reports from Japan announced the surrender offer before official notification reached Washington by way of Switzerland. At nine o'clock Stimson was called to the White House where the President was holding a conference on the surrender terms. All those present seemed eager to make the most of this great opportunity to end the war, but there was some doubt as to the propriety of accepting the Japanese condition.

" 'The President then asked me what my opinion was and I told him that I thought that even if the question hadn't been raised by the Japanese we would have to continue the Emperor ourselves under our command and supervision in order to get into surrender the many scattered armies of the Japanese who would own no other authority and that something like this use of the Emperor must be made in order to save us from a score of bloody Iwo Jimas and Okinawas all over China and the New Netherlands. He was the only source of authority in Japan under the Japanese theory of the State.' (Diary, August 10, 1945)

"The meeting at the White House soon adjourned to await the official surrender terms. Meanwhile Secretary Byrnes drafted a reply to which Stimson gave his prompt approval. In a later meeting this masterful paper was accepted by the President; it avoided any direct acceptance of the Japanese condition, but accomplished the desired purpose of reassuring the Japanese."

Suzuki's reply was typical of oriental methods **[1426/1427]** in retaining his supposed bargaining position until he knew precisely what the Potsdam Proclamation meant in that respect. The Asiatic concern over the loss of assumed bargaining power that might arise from exhibiting what might be **[1427/1428]** interpreted as a sign of weakness is always uppermost in Japanese mental processes. He can seldom be made to realize that the time for compromise has passed if it ever existed. This explains but certainly does not excuse Suzuki's reply, and the result of his reply was to release the atom bomb to fulfill its appointed purpose. Yet I and a good many others will always feel that had the President issued as far back as May, 1945, the recommended categorical statement that the Japanese dynasty would be retained if the Japanese people freely desired its retention, the atom bomb might never have had to be used at all. . . ."

. . . .

"A Thousand Years of Regret"*

LEWIS LICHTENSTEIN STRAUSS (1896-), financier and philanthropist, served in a number of posts in the Navy Department before and during World War II. He became special assistant to Secretary of the Navy James Forrestal in August, 1944, and from this position he was able to observe the high-level policymaking connected with the war against Japan. After the war he was appointed one of the original members of the Atomic Energy Commission. Although Admiral Strauss did not play a direct part in the decision to bomb Hiroshima, he was in close touch with the military events preceding the decision. This selection from his memoirs includes the minority statement by Under Secretary of the Navy Ralph Bard, the one member of President Truman's Interim Committee who dissented from the recommendation to use the bomb without warning.

. . . .

. . . [W]eeks before the date of the Alamogordo test, the war in the Pacific was already in its final stages, and the Japanese Government knew that they faced defeat. The Japanese High Command had been aware of it for months. It was not a secret in Washington, either. Two weeks earlier than the Alamogordo test the Secretary of War had informed the President that the Japanese Navy "is nearly destroyed and she is vulnerable to surface and underwater blockade which can deprive her of sufficient food and supplies for her population. She is terribly vulnerable to our concentrated air attack upon her crowded cities, industrial and food resources." He was inclined to think that it would be well worth while to give the Japanese warning of what was to come and definite opportunity to capitulate.

Fleet Admiral Ernest J. King, Commander in Chief of the United States Fleet and Chief of Naval Operations, in his final report to Secretary Forrestal noted:

> . . . when she [Japan] surrendered . . . her Navy had been destroyed and her Merchant Fleet had been fatally crippled. Dependent upon imported food and raw materials and relying upon sea transport to support her Armies at home and overseas, Japan lost the war because she lost command of the sea, and in doing so lost—to us—the island bases from which her factories and cities could be destroyed by air. . . . of twelve [Japanese] battleships, eleven were sunk; of twenty-six carriers, twenty were sunk; of forty-three cruisers, thirty-eight were destroyed; etc. throughout the various types of ships which collectively constituted a fleet considerably larger than ours was before the war. The few ships that remained afloat were for the most part so heavily damaged as to be of no military value.
>
> . . . After Okinawa was in our hands, the Japanese were in a desperate situation, which could be alleviated only if they could strike a counterblow either by damaging our fleet or by driving us from our advanced island position. The inability of the Japanese to do either was strong evidence of their increasing impotence and indicated that the end could not be long delayed. **[186/187]**

Between July 10 and August 6, the forces under Admiral Halsey's command had destroyed or damaged 2804 enemy

* Lewis L. Strauss, from "'A Thousand Years of Regret,'" *Men and Decisions* (New York: Doubleday and Co., 1962), pp. 186-195, 437-439.

planes and sunk or damaged 148 Japanese combat ships and 1598 merchant ships. "This impressive record," Admiral King observed, "speaks for itself and helps to explain the sudden collapse of Japan's will to resist.

> . . . While the damage to their cities and production centers by strategic bombing was fully as great as photographic reconnaissance had indicated, the strangulation from our less obvious, but relentlessly effective surface and submarine blockade and from our carrier-based air attacks had been a decisive factor in the enemy's collapse. Their Merchant Marine had been reduced to a fraction of its former size; of the few remaining ships, mostly small ones, only half were still operable. Their food situation was critical, and their remaining resources in fuel and all strategic materials were not less so. It had been known that their few remaining carriers and heavy Navy vessels had been damaged, but it appeared that the fury of our carrier strikes had forced them to withdraw all but a handful of men from these ships, practically abandoning them.

There were plans, well advanced, for landing our troops on the main Japanese islands in the autumn. Nevertheless, the Secretary of War also informed the President that if we were to effect a landing on one of the main islands and begin a forceful occupation of Japan, we should probably find that we had cast the die of last-ditch resistance. Fleet Admiral Nimitz was confident that *neither invasion nor atomic bombing* was required to produce surrender. He commented that our Pacific fleet was pounding Japan "with complete immunity." Japan was out of fuel. The battered remnant of her Navy had taken refuge of sorts in the Inland Sea. Secretary Stimson wrote that the attempt to exterminate Japan's armies and her population by gunfire "*or other means*" (the bomb was seldom mentioned in a memorandum except obliquely) would tend to produce a fussion of race solidity and antipathy.[9][**187/188**]

. . . .

The United States had, beside these individual judgments, one clear open window on Japan—our ability to intercept and rapidly decipher practically every communication between the Japanese Foreign Office and the Emperor's ambassadors overseas. We knew, accordingly, that the Japanese not only believed that they were beaten, they wanted to get out of the war as quickly as possible.

Admiral Joseph R. Redman, Chief of Naval Communications, brought to my office on July 13 an intercepted and decoded message from the Gaimusho (the Japanese Foreign Office) to Ambassador Sato in Moscow. It was signed by Togo, the Foreign Minister, and it instructed the Ambassador to call on Molotov at once before the Russians took off for Potsdam, where the Big Three, President Truman, Prime Minister Churchill, and Marshal Stalin were to meet. Sato was directed to lay before Molotov the earnest wish of the Emperor to see the end of the war. There were some pious expressions about the cessation of bloodshed, followed by a statement that Japan was prepared to forgo retention of territories she had conquered.

Later intercepts grew more desperate as Sato reported that he could not get to Molotov and had to content himself with interviews with a deputy, Lozovsky, who continually put him off with diplomatic double talk. On July 15, Sato's dispatch made it clear how well aware he was that Japan was utterly and completely defeated.

Forrestal, of course, saw the intercepts as they were received. We frequently read them together. He noted in his diary that Russian intervention to end the war was being sought even before there could have been much effect from the thousand-plane bombing raids of the Third Fleet and the naval bombardment of Kamaishi. As rapidly as they were received, Forrestal sent the intercepts to Admiral Leahy, the President's Chief of Staff, and later took the whole collection with him to Potsdam. He had not been invited to attend the Potsdam Conference, but he shared the view of former Ambassador Joseph C. Grew, our wisest and most experienced

Far Eastern diplomat, that if permitted to retain the Emperor the Japanese would agree to what, in every other respect, would be the "unconditional" surrender we sought.

Having decided that his responsibilities warranted him to "kibitz" (as he put it), Forrestal went to Potsdam without the grace of an invita- [188/189] tion. He did not fly there directly. Wishing his appearance to appear casual and in the course of other business, he stopped over in Paris on July 27, calling on Ambassador Jefferson Caffrey and attending to certain Navy business and did not reach Potsdam until the twenty-eighth. An irreversible entropy of events had occurred before his plane touched down.

Immediately on arrival he took the file of intercepted messages to Secretary Byrnes, who then saw them "in detail" for the first time. The Secretary of State had only been sworn in on July 3. On July 6 he had left for Potsdam, and the intervening day of briefing was almost entirely devoted to the issues on the Potsdam agenda. These related to the Allied positions on the defeat of Germany. He had not previously seen the texts of the messages.[10]

One message carried by Forrestal had been intercepted as recently as July 25. It was an instruction from the Japanese Foreign Minister to the Japanese Ambassador in Moscow. He was to go to any place that Molotov might designate and while still maintaining "unconditional surrender" to be unacceptable, to state that Japan had "no objection to a peace based on the Atlantic Charter" and that the terms requested by Japan were only those necessary to "secure and maintain our nation's existence and honor." The message mentioned the imminence of "complete collapse" and could only be read as having been prepared in an atmosphere of desperation.

Forrestal was too late by forty-eight hours. The Potsdam Declaration—the ultimatum to Japan—had been dispatched on the twenty-sixth, and events were now in the saddle, riding the decision makers.

On August 2, there was another intercept. "The battle situation has become acute," it understated. "There are only a few days left in which to make arrangements to end the war. . . . Since the loss of one day relative to this present matter may result in a thousand years of regret, it is requested that you immediately have a talk with Molotov." [189/190]

. . . .

On July 25 the President had made his decision. His orders had gone out to the Pacific, and on the little island of Tinian the special bomber group which long had trained to handle the bombs made its final preparations. Some months earlier a few officers especially cleared for the purpose had reviewed the maps of Japanese cities and selected a number of them as prospective targets. A committee of officers had been sent out to Los Alamos, where they conferred with Dr. J. Robert Oppenheimer, the director of the laboratory, and some of his associates. Dr. Oppenheimer was to testify nine years later that "Hiroshima was of course very successful partly for reasons unanticipated by us. We had been over the targets with a committee that was sent to consult us and to consider them, and the targets that were bombed were among the list that seemed bright to us."[12]

One individual had a negative voice in the choice of targets for the bomb. Among the cities initially selected for the bombing had been Kyoto. Secretary Stimson, when he learned of it, interposed his personal veto. I had visited Kyoto in 1926 and could appreciate his reasons. Kyoto was the cultural and religious center of old Japan. There were located the delicately beautiful palaces of the former emperors who held court in exile while the country was governed by the warlike shoguns in Tokyo. There were the hundreds of ancient temples and shrines fashioned of carved and gilded wood. Destruction of Kyoto would [190/191] have added vandalism to whatever charge might be leveled against the target selections.

About a recommendation which had been made that instead of exploding the bomb over an inhabited city it should be demonstrated over some unpopulated area, the laboratory group said that they "did not think exploding one of these things as a firecracker over a desert was likely to be very impressive."[13]

Einstein and Szilard sought unsuccessfully to arrest the course of events. . . . A . . . second letter to President Roosevelt was written by Dr. Einstein and is reported to have been found unopened among the President's mail in Warm Springs, Georgia, at the time of his death in April 1945.[14]

The letter requested an appointment for Dr. Szilard to propose certain considerations and recommendations which "unusual circumstances" persuaded Einstein should be brought to the attention of the President in spite of the fact that he did not know the substance of the considerations and recommendations which Szilard proposed to submit. This was due to the fact that security prevented Szilard from any disclosures to Einstein. Einstein concluded with the statement that he understood Szilard was greatly concerned about the lack of adequate contact between the scientists who were working on the project and the members of the President's cabinet who were responsible for formulating policy.

When President Truman received the letter, he referred it to Secretary Byrnes with the request that the Secretary see Dr. Szilard, who, in company with Drs. Urey and Walter Bartky, called on him at his home in Spartanburg, South Carolina, on May 28. When they left, Secretary Byrnes gave them Dr. Einstein's letter, which Szilard duly returned to the President's secretary. Secretary Byrnes has recorded that, as Dr. Einstein's letter had forecast, Szilard "complained that he and some of his associates did not know enough about the policy of the Government with regard to the use of the bomb." Secretary Byrnes did not react favorably to the suggestion that discussion between the scientists and the policy-makers at Cabinet level should be initiated. In the course of his presentation, Byrnes recalled that Szilard had said that the younger scientists were very critical of Drs. Bush, Compton, and Conant, who were among the senior scientific advisers to the President. Byrnes told the delegation that Dr. Oppenheimer would be consulted about the use of the bomb, which assurance appeared to satisfy them.[15] **[191/192]**

Under Secretary Ralph Bard represented the Navy Department on the Interdepartmental Committee on Atomic Energy (Army, Navy, State) and forthrightly committed his views to the record at the time:

27 June 1945

MEMORANDUM ON THE USE OF S-1 BOMB

Ever since I have been in touch with this program I have had a feeling that before the bomb is actually used against Japan that Japan should have some preliminary warning for say two or three days in advance of use. The position of the United States as a great humanitarian nation and the fair play attitude of our people generally is responsible in the main for this feeling.

During recent weeks I have also had the feeling very definitely that the Japanese Government may be searching for some opportunity which they could use as a medium of surrender. Following the three-power conference emissaries from this country could contact representatives from Japan somewhere on the China Coast and make representations with regard to Russia's position and at the same time give them some information regarding the proposed use of atomic power, together with whatever assurances the President might care to make with regard to the Emperor of Japan and the treatment of the Japanese nation following unconditional surrender. It seems quite possible to me that this presents the opportunity which the Japanese are looking for.

I don't see that we have anything in particular to lose in following such a program. The stakes are so tremendous that it is my opinion very real consideration should be given to some plan of this kind. I do not believe under present circumstances existing that there is anyone in this country whose evaluation of the chances of the success of such a program is worth a great deal. The only way to find out is to try it out.

/s/ Ralph A. Bard

Dr. Arthur H. Compton, the Nobel laureate in physics, who had contributed so outstandingly to the war effort, also raised the question of whether it might not be possible to arrange a demonstration of the bomb, "in such a manner that the Japanese will be so impressed that they would see the uselessness of continuing the war."[16]

I had made a suggestion to Secretary Forrestal that the power of the bomb be displayed as a warning in an uninhabited area. It seemed to me that a demonstration over a forest would offer impressive evidence to show the terrible effect of enormous blast and heat. A meteor which [**192/193**] fell near Lake Baikal in Siberia in 1908 had knocked down forests for miles around its point of impact and the trees lay in windrows radiating like the spokes of a wheel from the center. I recalled a grove of cryptomeria trees near the little village of Nikko on the main Japanese island. This seemed to me a place where an impressive demonstration could be made. The inhabitants, priests, and shrine servants could be warned to evacuate beforehand. It troubled me to think of using what might turn out to be a cataclysmic weapon over a crowded Japanese metropolis of wood-and-paper houses and multitudes of women and children in a defeated nation.

In justification for the rejection of these proposals it has since been argued that even the first test in New Mexico was not sufficient to assure that the weapon would explode when dropped from an airplane. This was because the system for detonating the bomb at a predetermined altitude had not been proved at Alamogordo, where the bomb was fixed on the top of a steel tower. This argument was furnished to Secretary Stimson, who restated it in a magazine article in 1947. The fusing system had been repeatedly and successfully tested, however. This specific justification against a demonstration seemed to me of little validity.

Secretary Forrestal recorded a conversation which he had with John J. McCloy in March of 1947. McCloy had recalled a meeting with President Truman in the summer of 1945, before Potsdam. McCloy had volunteered his views, which were that the Japanese should be told that we had perfected a terrifyingly destructive weapon which we would have to use if they did not surrender. He had said that some of the Japanese who had been in Germany during our bombing raids were now back in Japan and could testify to the devastation they had seen produced by conventional weapons. We should add, McCloy said, that the Japanese would be permitted to retain the Emperor and a form of government of their own choosing. Forrestal noted that McCloy observed that the military leaders were somewhat annoyed at his interference but that the President welcomed it. At the conclusion of McCloy's comments, the President had "ordered such a political offensive to be set in motion."[17] The offensive greatly strengthened the hands of the peace party in Japan but was eclipsed.

General Eisenhower was in Potsdam at this period, but, the war in Europe being over, he had not been invited as a participant in the conference. Secretary Stimson told him, however, about the test at Alamogordo and described his relief that it had been successful. He indi- [**193/194**] cated his keen sense of personal responsibility. General Eisenhower expressed the hope that we would never have to use such a weapon against an enemy because he disliked seeing the United States "initiate the use" of anything so horrible and destructive.[18]

The voices recommending restraint were crying in the wilderness. [**194/195**]

. . . .

Mr. Churchill recalls that at Potsdam . . . "there never was a moment's discussion as to whether the atomic bomb should be used or not," adding, "The historic fact remains, and must be judged in the after time, that the *decision whether or not to use the atomic bomb to compel the surrender of Japan was never an issue.* . . . There was unanimous, automatic, unquestioned agreement around our table; nor did I ever hear the slightest suggestion that we should do otherwise." (Italics supplied.)[19] [195/437]

. . . .

[9] Stimson, Henry L., and Bundy, McGeorge, *On Active Service in Peace and War,* Harper & Brothers, 1949, page 635, [622].

[10] Brynes, James F., *All in One Lifetime,* Harper & Brothers, 1958, page 297.

Forrestal, James V., *Diaries,* Viking Press, 1951, page 78.

Secretary Brynes in a letter to the writer states, "It is understandable that at that time I did not know all the details, because I had only become Secretary on July 3, 1945. The following day was a holiday and we left Washington the evening of the 6th. I was in the Department only two working days, July 5th and 6th. We anticipated little discussion at Potsdam about the Japanese phase of the war and in those two days we concentrated on the subjects incident to winding up the European conflict, which were on the agenda."

According to Herbert Feis . . . "the State Department historians who collected and edited the Potsdam papers have not found it possible to establish precisely which of the messages (in translation) were read by Stimson and other members of the American civilian and military groups while they were in Potsdam, nor precisely when they were informed of the contents of [437/438] particular messages." Feis, Herbert, *Japan Subdued,* Princeton University Press, 1961, page 57, footnote.

. . . .

[12] In the Matter of J. Robert Oppenheimer, Texts of Principal Documents and Letters of the Personnel Security Board, General Manager, and Commissioners, Washington, D.C., May 27, 1954, through June 29, 1954, page 33, United States Government Printing Office, Washington, D.C., 1954.

[13] *Ibid.,* page 34.

[14] Letter from Albert Einstein to President Roosevelt, dated March 25, 1945.

112 Mercer Street
Princeton, New Jersey
March 25, 1945

The Honorable Franklin Delano Roosevelt
The President of the United States
The White House
Washington, D.C.

Sir:

I am writing you to introduce Dr. L. Szilard who proposes to submit to you certain considerations and recommendations. Unusual circumstances which I shall describe further below induce me to take this action in spite of the fact that I do not know the substance of the considerations and recommendations which Dr. Szilard proposes to submit to you.

In the summer of 1939 Dr. Szilard put before me his views concerning the potential importance of uranium for national defense. He was greatly disturbed by the potentialities involved and anxious that the United States Government be advised of them as soon as possible. Dr. Szilard, who is one of the discoverers of the neutron emission of uranium on which all present work on uranium is based, described to me a specific system which he devised and which he thought would make it possible to set up a chain reaction in unseparated uranium in the immediate future. Having known him for over twenty years both from his scientific work and personally, I have much confidence in his judgment and it was on the basis of his judgment as well as my own that I took the liberty to approach you in connection with this subject. You responded to my letter dated August 2, 1939 by the appointment of a committee under the chairmanship of Dr. Briggs and thus started the Government's activity in this field.

The terms of secrecy under which Dr. Szilard is working at present do not permit him to give me information about his work; however, I understand that he now is greatly concerned about the lack of adequate contact between scientists who are doing this work and those members of your Cabinet who are responsible for formulating policy. In the circumstances I consider it my duty to give Dr. Szilard this introduction and I wish to express the hope that you will be able to give his presentation of the case your personal attention.

Very truly yours,

A. Einstein

[15] Byrnes, James F., *All in One Lifetime,* page 284.

[16] Compton, Arthur H., *Atomic Quest; a Personal Narrative,* Oxford University Press, 1956, pages 238-39. [438/439]

[17] Forrestal, *op. cit.,* page 71.

[18] Eisenhower, Dwight D., *Crusade in Europe,* Doubleday & Company, Inc., 1948, page 443.

[19] Churchill, Sir Winston, *Triumph and Tragedy,* Doubleday & Company, Inc., 1953, page 639.

Choosing the Target*

LESLIE RICHARD GROVES (1896-), brigadier general in the Army Corps of Engineers, was in charge of the Manhattan Engineering District from 1942 to 1946. In this position General Groves was the man most directly responsible for organizing the entire project through which the first atomic bombs were produced. Among the aspects of the Manhattan Project that have aroused controversy since the war were the extensive security arrangements in effect throughout the organization. This issue is discussed in the article by Fletcher Knebel and Charles Bailey, reprinted on pages 63-67.

There has been much discussion since the war about the decision to use the atomic bomb against Japan. Decisions of this nature must always be made by only one man, and, in this case, the burden fell upon President Truman. Under the terms of the Quebec Agreement, the concurrence of Prime Minister Churchill was necessary; nevertheless, the initial decision and the primary responsibility were Mr. Truman's. As far as I was concerned, his decision was one of noninterference—basically, a decision not to upset the existing plans.

When we first began to develop atomic energy, the United States was in no way committed to employ atomic weapons against any other power. With the activation of the Manhattan Project, however, the situation began to change. Our work was extremely costly, both in money and in its interference with the rest of the war effort. As time went on, and as we poured more and more money and effort into the project, the government became increasingly committed to the ultimate use of the bomb, and while it has often been said that we undertook development of this terrible weapon so that Hitler would not get it first, the fact remains that the original decision to make the project an all-out effort was based upon using it to end the war. As Mr. Stimson succinctly put it, the Manhattan Project existed "to bring the war to a successful end more quickly than otherwise would be the case and thus to save American lives."

Certainly, there was no question in my mind, or, as far as I was ever aware, in the mind of either President Roosevelt or President Truman or any other responsible person, but that we were developing a weapon to be employed against the enemies of the United States. The first serious mention of the possibility that the atomic bomb might not be used came after V-E Day, when Under Secretary of War Patterson asked me whether the surrender in Europe might not alter our plans for dropping the bomb on Japan.

I said that I could see no reason why the decision taken by President Roosevelt when he approved the tremendous effort involved in the Manhattan Project should be changed for that reason, since the surrender of Germany had in no way lessened Japan's activities against the United States. A little later some of the scientists began to express [**265/266**] doubts about the desirability of using the bomb against

* Leslie R. Groves, from "Choosing the Target," *Now It Can Be Told: The Story of the Manhattan Project* (New York: Harper & Brothers, 1961), pp. 265-266. Reprinted with the permission of Harper & Row, Publishers, Inc.

Japan. A number of these men had come to the United States to escape racial persecution under the Hitler regime. To them, Hitler was the supreme enemy and, once he had been destroyed, they apparently found themselves unable to generate the same degree of enthusiasm for destroying Japan's military power.

At this same time a debate arose about how the bomb should be employed. Should we conduct a demonstration of its power for all the world to see, and then deliver an ultimatum to Japan, or should we use it without warning? It was always difficult for me to understand how anyone could ignore the importance of the effect on the Japanese people and their government of the overwhelming surprise of the bomb. To achieve surprise was one of the reasons we had tried so hard to maintain our security.

President Truman knew of these diverse and conflicting opinions. He must have engaged in some real soul-searching before reaching his final decision. In my opinion, his resolve to continue with the original plan will always stand as an act of unsurpassed courage and wisdom—courage because, for the first time in the history of the United States, the President personally determined the course of a major military strategical and tactical operation for which he could be considered directly responsible; and wisdom because history, if any thought is given to the value of American lives, has conclusively proven that his decision was correct.

. . . .

PART TWO
THE SCIENTISTS

*In the Matter of J. Robert Oppenheimer**

Since 1947 J. Robert Oppenheimer (1904-) has been director and professor of physics at the Institute for Advanced Study in Princeton, New Jersey. From 1943 to 1945 he served as director of the laboratory at Los Alamos, New Mexico, where the atomic bomb was actually built. He was also a member of the scientific advisory panel to the Interim Committee which President Truman appointed to make recommendations concerning the use of the bomb. A decade later Dr. Oppenheimer was denied security clearance by the Atomic Energy Commission. The first part of the selection which follows is part of a letter of March 4, 1954 from Dr. Oppenheimer to General K. D. Nichols, General Manager of the Atomic Energy Commission. The letter was read into the hearings conducted by the commission's Personnel Security Board. In addition to the letter, Dr. Oppenheimer answered a number of questions in which he recalled the attitudes among scientists connected with the wartime atomic energy project.

. . . .

"THE WAR YEARS

"Ever since the discovery of nuclear fission, the possibility of powerful explosives based on it had been very much in my mind, as it had in that of many other physicists. We had some understanding of what this might do for us in the war, and how much it might change the course of history. In the autumn of 1941, a special committee was set up by the National Academy of Sciences under the chairmanship of Arthur Compton to review the prospects and feasibility of the different uses of atomic energy for military purposes. I attended a meeting of this committee; this was my first official connection with the atomic-energy program. **[11/12]**

. . . .

"In early 1943, I received a letter signed by General Groves and Dr. Conant, appointing me director of the laboratory, and outlining their conception of how it was to be organized and administered. The necessary construction and assembling of the needed facilities were begun. All of us worked in close colloboration with the engineers of the Manhattan District.

"The site of Los Alamos was selected, in part at least, because it enabled those responsible to balance the obvious need for security with the equally important need of free communication among those engaged in the work. Security, it was hoped, would be achieved by removing the laboratory to a remote area, fenced and patrolled, where communication with the outside was extremely limited. Telephone calls were monitored, mail was censored, and personnel who left the area—something permitted only for the clearest of causes—knew that their movements might be under surveillance. On the other hand, for those within the community, fullest exposition and discussion among those competent to use the information was encouraged.

"The last months of 1942 and early 1943 had hardly hours enough to get Los Alamos established. The real problem

*** United States Atomic Energy Commission, from *In the Matter of J. Robert Oppenheimer,* Transcript of Hearing before Personnel Security Board, April 12, 1954, through May 6, 1954 (Washington, D. C., 1954), pp. 11-15, 31-33.**

had to do with getting to Los Alamos the men who would make a success of the undertaking. For this we needed to understand as clearly as we then could what our technical program would be, what men we would need, what facilities, what organization, what plan.

"The program of recruitment was massive. Even though we then underestimated the ultimate size of the laboratory, which was to have almost 4,000 members by the spring of 1945, and even though we did not at that time see clearly some of the difficulties which were to bedevil and threaten the enterprise, we knew that it was a big, complex and diverse job. Even the initial plan of the laboratory called for a start with more than 100 highly qualified and trained scientists, to say nothing of the technicians, staff, and mechanics who would be required for their support, and of the equipment that we would have to beg and borrow since there would be no time to build it from scratch. We had to recruit at a time when the country was fully engaged in war and almost every competent scientist was already involved in the military effort.

"The primary burden of this fell on me. To recruit staff I traveled all over the country talking with people who had been working on one or another aspect of the atomic-energy enterprise, and people in radar work, for example, and underwater sound, telling them about the job, the place that we were going to, and enlisting their enthusiasm.

"In order to bring responsible scientists to Los Alamos, I had to rely on their sense of the interest, urgency, and feasibility of the Los Alamos mission. I had to tell them enough of what the job was, and give strong enough assurance that it might be successfully accomplished in time to affect the outcome of the war, to make it clear that they were justified in their leaving other work to come to this job.

"The prospect of coming to Los Alamos aroused great misgivings. It was to be a military post; men were asked to sign up more or less for the duration; restrictions on travel and on the freedom of families to move about to be severe; and no one could be sure of the extent to which the necessary technical freedom **[12/13]** of action could actually be maintained by the laboratory. The notion of disappearing into the New Mexico desert for an indeterminate period and under quasi military auspices disturbed a good many scientists, and the families of many more. But there was another side to it. Almost everyone realized that this was a great undertaking. Almost everyone knew that if it were completed successfully and rapidly enough, it might determine the outcome of the war. Almost everyone knew that it was an unparalleled opportunity to bring to bear the basic knowledge and art of science for the benefit of his country. Almost everyone knew that this job, if it were achieved, would be a part of history. This sense of excitement, of devotion and of patriotism in the end prevailed. Most of those with whom I talked came to Los Alamos. Once they came, confidence in the enterprise grew as men learned more of the technical status of the work; and though the laboratory was to double and redouble its size many times before the end, once it had started it was on the road to success.

"We had information in those days of German activity in the field of nuclear fission. We were aware of what it might mean if they beat us to the draw in the development of atomic bombs. The consensus of all our opinions, and every directive that I had, stressed the extreme urgency of our work, as well as the need for guarding all knowledge of it from our enemies. Past Communist connections or sympathies did not necessarily disqualify a man from employment, if we had confidence in his integrity and dependability as a man. **[13/14]**

. . . .

"The story of Los Alamos is long and complex. Part of it is public history. For me it was a time so filled with work, with the need for decision and action and consultation, that there was room for little else. I lived with my family in the community which was Los Alamos. It was a remarkable community, inspired by a high sense of mission, of duty and of destiny, coherent, dedicated, and remarkably selfless. There was plenty in the life of Los Alamos to cause irritation; the security restrictions, many of my own devising, the inadequacies and inevitable fumblings of a military post unlike any that had ever existed before, shortages, inequities, and in the laboratory itself the shifting emphasis on different aspects of the technical work as the program moved forward; but I have never known a group more understanding and more devoted to a common purpose, more willing to lay aside personal convenience and prestige, more understanding of the role that they were playing in their country's history. Time and again we had in the technical work almost paralyzing crises. Time and again the laboratory drew itself together and faced the new problems and got on with the work. We worked by night and by day; and in the end the many jobs were done.

"These years of hard and loyal work of the scientists culminated in the test on July 16, 1945. It was a success. I believe that in the eyes of the War Department, and other knowledgeable people, it was as early a success as they had thought possible, given all the circumstances, and rather a greater one. There were many indications from the Secretary of War and General Groves, and many others, that official opinion was one of satisfaction with what had been accomplished. At the time, it was hard for us in Los Alamos not to share that satisfaction, and hard for me not to accept the conclusion that I had managed the enterprise well and played a key part in its success. But it needs to be stated that many others contributed the decisive ideas and carried out the work which led to this success and that my role was that of understanding, encouraging, suggesting and deciding. It was the very opposite of a one-man show.

"Even before the July 16 test and the use of the bombs in Japan, the members of the laboratory began to have a new sense of the possible import of what was going on. In the early days, when success was less certain and timing unsure, and the war with Germany and Japan in a desperate phase, it was enough for us to think that we had a job to do. Now, with Germany defeated, the war in the Pacific approaching a crisis, and the success of our undertaking almost assured, there was a sense both of hope and of anxiety as to what this spectacular development might portend for the future. This came to us a little earlier than to the public generally because we saw the technical development at close range and in secret; but its quality was very much the same as the public response after Hiroshima and Nagasaki.

"Thus it was natural that in the spring of 1945 I welcomed the opportunity when I was asked by Secretary Stimson to serve, along with Compton, Lawrence, and Fermi, on an advisory panel to his Interim Committee on Atomic Energy. We met with that committee on the 1st of June 1945; and even during the week **[14/15]** when Hiroshima and Nagasaki were being bombed, we met at Los Alamos to sketch out a prospectus of what the technical future in atomic energy might look like: atomic war heads for guided missiles, improvements in bomb designs, the thermonuclear program, power, propulsion, and the new tools available from atomic technology for research in science, medicine, and technology. This work absorbed much of my time, during September and October; and in connection with it I was asked to consult with the War and State Departments on atomic-energy legislation, and in a preliminary way on the international control of atomic energy.

"I resigned as director of Los Alamos on October 16, 1945, after having secured the consent of Commander Bradbury and General Groves that Bradbury should act as my successor. **[15/31]**

. . . .

By Mr. GARRISON [Lloyd K. Garrison, counsel for Dr. Oppenheimer]:

. . . .

Q. As the work progressed, you began to get goals and deadlines, I suppose, against which to produce the bomb, if you could?

A. The deadline never changed. It was as soon as possible. This depends on when we were ready, when the stuff was ready, and how much stuff we needed.

Q. Wasn't there a particular effort to get it done before the Potsdam Conference?

A. Yes, that was of course quite late. After the collapse of Germany, we understood that it was important to get this ready for the war in Japan. We were told that it would be very important—I was told I guess by Mr. Stimson—that it would be very important to know the state of affairs before the meeting at Potsdam at which the future conduct of the war in the Far East would be discussed.

Q. Discussed with the Russians?

A. I don't want to overstate that. It was my understanding, and on the morning of July 16, I think Dr. Bush told me, that it was the intention of the United States statesmen who went to Potsdam to say something about this to the Russians. I never knew how much. Mr. Stimson explained later that he had planned to say a good deal more than what was said, but when they saw what the Russians looked like and how it felt, he didn't know whether it was a good idea. The historical record as it is published indicates that the President said no more than we had a new weapon which we planned to use in Japan, and it was very powerful. I believe we were under incredible pressure to get it done before the Potsdam meeting and Groves and I bickered for a couple of days. [**31/32**] But in actual time it has been done enough times. There have been enough lurid news stories about that first test so that I need not repeat what it was like. In other context it should be said that it was as successful as we had any reason to hope, and I believe we got the job done as fast as we could. That is what we were told to do.

Mr. Garrison. At this point I would like to read into the record a letter from General Groves——

Mr. Robb [counsel for the Board]. May I enquire, Mr. Garrison, these are copies, but you have the originals available?

Mr. Garrison. We have the originals available and we would be very glad to show them to you.

Mr. Robb. Thank you.

Mr. Garrison. This is the letter of July 19, 1945, from General Groves and [*sic*] Dr. Oppenheimer reading as follows: [Reading:]

"Since I returned to Washington I have done little else but think about and talk about the truly magnificent results of the test conducted at Trinity last Monday morning."

Trinity was the code name for the place.

The Witness. Yes.

Mr. Garrison (reading): "As time goes on and the test begins to take on its true perspective, I appreciate more and more the outstanding performance of you and your people in making the test so successful.

"General Farrell and I have discussed the project in all its many phases and have reviewed it from every possible angle. We both feel that the job is a high-water mark of scientific and engineering performance. Your leadership and skill and the loyal and able performance of all your subordinates made it possible.

"An immediate report was cabled to the Secretary of War on Monday on the great performance."

That would be to Potsdam, I take it?

The Witness. Yes.

Mr. Garrison (reading): "He promptly cabled back heartiest congratulations to all concerned. This morning a fuller written report was sent to him by special courier and he should have our impressions of the test by the time you get this letter. I know that the President, the Secretaries of State and War and General Marshall who are so importantly engaged at Potsdam now will be as tremendously impressed as we were by the results of the test.

"I hope you will show or read the suitable parts of this letter to the men who did so much to make the job go so well and that you will extend to them my grateful thanks for a job well done.

"Again, with deepest thanks and every good wish for the continued success of our great project from both General Farrell and myself, I am,

Sincerely yours,

L. R. GROVES,
Major General, USA."

The WITNESS. Now, there are a few points I might make about this period.

. . . .

. . . Mr. Garrison has asked me . . . whether there was any change in tempo after the war against Germany ended. There was, but it was upward. It was upward simply because we were still more frantic to have the job done and wanted to have it done so that if needed, it would be available.

In any case, we wanted to have it done before the war was over, and nothing much could be done. I don't think there was any time where we worked harder [**32/33**] at the speedup than in the period after the German surrender and the actual combat use of the bomb.

. . . I did suggest to General Groves some changes in bomb design which would make more efficient use of the material; and they have long since been done, of course. He turned them down as jeopardizing the promptness of the availability of bombs. He and I may not entirely agree about how long a delay would have been involved, but the very fact that any delay was involved was unacceptable.

Finally, there was, of course, a great deal of discussion—and I will return to the formal aspects of that—about the desirability of using the bombs in Japan. I think the hotbed of this discussion was in Chicago rather than in Los Alamos. At Los Alamos I heard very little talk about it. We always assumed, if they were needed, they would be used. But there were places where people said for the future of the world it would be better not to use them.

This problem was referred to me in a capacity different than director of Los Alamos. We did everything we could to get them out there and as fast and smooth as possible.

There was, however, at Los Alamos a change in the feel of people. I am talking vaguely because this is a community now of seven or eight thousand people, of whom maybe 1,000 or more are scientists and very close to each other, talking all the time. This was partly a war measure, but it was also something that was here to stay. There was a great sense of uncertainty and anxiety about what should be done about it.

The generation of that kind of public—of a concern very similar to the public concern—that followed Hiroshima and one natural outgrowth of which was our abortive effort to establish quite a new relation among nations in the control of atomic energy; that was not something that had its roots very far back; it started toward the end when the war was about over.

Hiroshima was, of course, very successful, partly for reasons unanticipated by us. We had been over the targets with a committee that was sent out to consult us and to consider them, and the targets that were bombed were among the list that seemed bright to us.

The Secretary of War deleted one target, and I have always been glad he did. That was the unbombed and culture capital of Japan, Kyoto. He struck that off. The two that were hit were among the targets selected. We sent a mission on out from Los Alamos to assemble, test the bombs on Tinian, and to fly with the B-29's that went out over the targets, and also to go in as soon as they could get clearance from General MacArthur.

That mission was under General Farrell, who might appear—I am not sure he can—to see what mess we made of those two towns.

. . . .

Choice*

ARTHUR HOLLY COMPTON (1895-), Nobel prizewinner in physics (1927) and former chancellor of Washington University in St. Louis, was associated with the development of atomic weapons from the early days of World War II. In 1941 he served as chairman of the National Academy of Sciences' committee on the military use of atomic energy. From 1942 to 1945 he was director of the Metallurgical Laboratory at the University of Chicago, where the chain reaction was achieved that preceded the production of an atomic bomb. Dr. Compton was also a member of the scientific advisory panel that assisted President Truman's Interim Committee in reaching a recommendation on the use of the bomb.

'Gentlemen, it is our responsibility to recommend action that may turn the course of civilization. In our hands we expect soon to have a weapon of wholly unprecedented destructive power. Today's prime fact is war. Our great task is to bring this war to a prompt and successful conclusion. We may assume that our new weapon puts in our hands overwhelming power. It is our obligation to use this power with the best wisdom we can command. To us now the matter of first importance is how our use of this new weapon will appear in the long view of history.'

This, as accurately as I can recall it, was the statement made by Secretary of War Henry L. Stimson as he presented to the 'Interim Committee' the question of what should be done with the atomic bomb. The place was the Secretary's office in Washington. The date was 31 May 1945. . . . [**219/236**]

. . . .

THE INTERIM COMMITTEE CONSIDERS. After Secretary Stimson's opening statement at the meeting of 31 May 1945, he turned the committee's attention immediately to what the atomic bomb could do and how it might be used. Oppenheimer explained that the simplest kind of bomb was necessarily the objective of this first development. Such a bomb could be exploded above the ground with the help of the newly developed proximity fuse. Its greatest military effect would be in destroying structures by the blast of the explosion. The kind of target on which such a weapon would have the greatest military effect seemed to be either a concentration of troops or war plants whose buildings could be put out of commission by the explosion. Oppenheimer [**236/237**] noted that if the bomb were exploded over a city their estimates indicated that some 20,000 people would probably be killed.[7] He was giving a technical reply to a technical question. Stimson's response was that of a man of wide culture and broad sympathy, to whom Japan was a living reality. To him Japan was

[7] It was not anticipated that when the attack was made practically no one would have sought shelter. This was the major reason for the considerable error in this estimate when compared with the roughly 100,000 killed at Hiroshima and 40,000 at Nagasaki. The estimates were based on experience with previous bomb attacks. The deadly fire raids that caused such complete destruction in densely populated Tokyo took just as many lives. But, because the area of destruction in Tokyo was four times as great, the number of lives lost per square mile at Tokyo was only one-fourth as great as at Hiroshima and Nagasaki.

* Arthur H. Compton, from "Choice," *Atomic Quest* (New York: Oxford University Press, 1956), pp. 219, 236-244.

not just a place on the map, not only a nation that must be defeated. The objective was military damage, he pointed out, not civilian lives. To illustrate his point he noted that Kyoto was a city that must not be bombed. It lies in the form of a cup and thus would be exceptionally vulnerable. But this city, he said, is no military target. It is exclusively a place of homes and art and shrines.

General Marshall stated that from the point of view of the postwar safety of the nation he would have to argue against the use of the bomb in World War II, at least if its existence could be kept secret. Such use, he said, would show our hand. We would be in a stronger position with regard to future military action if we did not show the power we held.

This led to a discussion about the possibility of maintaining secrecy about our development of atomic weapons. The members of the Scientific Panel were unanimous in the opinion that so many persons already knew of the wartime atomic studies that soon after the war it would be common knowledge that nuclear energy could be released and that it could not be long before an atomic explosion would somewhere be tried.

This reply did not, however, answer fully General Marshall's [**237/238**] objection to the use of the bomb. Even though the knowledge of the availability of atomic energy might become widespread, perhaps the details of the bomb itself would not be known outside of the United States and Britain. In any case, if the bomb were not used in the present war the compelling incentive for its development by other nations would be lacking.

Though General Marshall was thus noting a real military objection to any demonstration of the bomb, he seemed to accept the view that its use was nevertheless important. This I verified in subsequent discussions. He was fully convinced at this time that the bomb should be used. This was primarily to bring the war quickly to a close and thereby to save lives. He never believed that the Japanese would surrender solely as a result of further naval operations and conventional air attacks. At this meeting, however, Marshall was careful to avoid any statement that might prejudice the thinking of the civilian committee. It was their verdict that was being sought as to whether the lives that the bomb might save were more or less important than the possible advantage of holding a powerful secret weapon.

Throughout the morning's discussions it seemed to be a foregone conclusion that the bomb would be used. It was regarding only the details of strategy and tactics that differing views were expressed. At the luncheon following the morning meeting, I was seated at Mr. Stimson's left. In the course of the conversation I asked the Secretary whether it might not be possible to arrange a nonmilitary demonstration of the bomb in such a manner that the Japanese would be so impressed that they would see the uselessness of continuing the war. The Secretary opened this question for general discussion by those at the table. Various possibilities were brought forward. One after the other it seemed necessary that they should be discarded.

It was evident that everyone would suspect trickery. If a bomb were exploded in Japan with previous notice, the Japanese air power was still adequate to give serious interference. An atomic [**238/239**] bomb was an intricate device, still in the developmental stage. Its operation would be far from routine. If during the final adjustments of the bomb the Japanese defenders should attack, a faulty move might easily result in some kind of failure. Such an end to an advertised demonstration of power would be much worse than if the attempt had not been made. It was now evident that when the time came for the bombs to be used we should have only one of them available, followed afterwards by others at all-too-long intervals. We could not afford the chance that one of them might be a dud. If the test were made on some neutral territory, it was hard to believe that Japan's determined and fanatical military men would be impressed. If such an open test were made first and failed to bring surrender, the chance would be gone to give the shock of surprise that proved so effective. On the contrary, it would make the Japanese ready to interfere with an atomic attack if they could. Though the possibility of a demonstration that would not destroy human lives was attractive, no one could suggest a way in which it could be made so convincing that it would be likely to stop the war.

After luncheon the Interim Committee went into executive session. Our Scientific Panel was then again invited in. We were asked to prepare a report as to whether we could devise any kind of demonstration that would seem likely to bring the war to an end without using the bomb against a live target.

Ten days later, at Oppenheimer's invitation, Lawrence, Fermi, and I spent a long week end at Los Alamos. We were keenly aware of our responsibility as the scientific advisers to the Interim Committee. Among our colleagues were the scientists who supported Franck in suggesting a nonmilitary demonstration only. We thought of the fighting men who were set for an invasion which would be so very costly in both American and Japanese lives. We were determined to find, if we could, some effective way of demonstrating the power of an atomic bomb without loss [**239/240**] of life that would impress Japan's warlords. If only this could be done!

Ernest Lawrence was the last one of our group to give up hope for finding such a solution. The difficulties of making a purely technical demonstration that would carry its impact effectively into Japan's controlling councils were indeed great. We had to count on every possible effort to distort even obvious facts. Experience with the determination of Japan's fighting men made it evident that the war would not be stopped unless these men themselves were convinced of its futility. Secretary Stimson has published the following paragraph which constituted the essence of our report:

> The opinions of our scientific colleagues on the initial use of these weapons are not unanimous: they range from the proposal of a purely technical demonstration to that of the military application best designed to induce surrender. Those who advocate a purely technical demonstration would wish to outlaw the use of atomic weapons, and have feared that if we use the weapons now our position in future negotiations will be prejudiced. Others emphasize the opportunity of saving American lives by immediate military use, and believe that such use will improve the international prospects, in that they are more concerned with the prevention of war than with the elimination of this special weapon. We find ourselves closer to these latter views; *we can propose no technical demonstration likely to bring an end to the war; we see no acceptable alternative to direct military use.* (The italics are Mr. Stimson's.)[8]

Our hearts were heavy as on 16 June we turned in this report to the Interim Committee. We were glad and proud to have had a part in making the power of the atom available for the [**240/241**] use of man. What a tragedy it was that this power should become available first in time of war and that it must first be used for human destruction. If, however, it would result in the shortening of the war and the saving of lives—if it would mean bringing us closer to the time when war would be abandoned as a means of settling international disputes—here must be our hope and our basis for courage.

PETITIONS AND POLLS. The statement of our Scientific Panel to the Interim Committee was in close accord with the views of most of the scientists engaged on the atomic project. The case against use of the bomb in the Japanese theater was pressed most vigorously by Leo Szilard. Fearful lest more routine procedures be ineffective, he wrote a letter direct to the President and went to Washington to urge personally that the use of the bomb be blocked. He circulated petitions at

[8] Stimson, Henry L., 'The Decision To Use the Atomic Bomb,' *Harper's Magazine* 194 (February 1947) 101.

Chicago and urged others to circulate similar petitions at Los Alamos and Oak Ridge requesting that the atomic bomb should not be used in World War II. This action stimulated counterpetitions requesting that as soon as the bombs were available they should be used as might be necessary to bring the war to a close.

There were few who sensed as clearly as did Szilard the shock that would be felt throughout the world if the atomic bomb destroyed large numbers of Japanese lives. This he thought of as an international crime and believed that many in all parts of the world would share this view. He had been willing to approve and even to urge the use of the bomb against the Germans, for in this case it would be an evil less than that of the human destruction he felt sure would result if the Nazis should gain the victory. He could not persuade himself that the case was the same with regard to the Japanese.

The first form of the petition circulated by Szilard called for outright rejection of the use of atomic bombs on moral considerations. The heart of his argument was this: [**241/242**]

> Once they were introduced as an instrument of war it would be difficult to resist the temptation of putting them to such use . . . Thus a nation which sets the precedent of using these newly liberated forces of nature for purposes of destruction may have to bear the responsibility of opening the door to an era of devastation on an unimaginable scale.

In this form of his petition Szilard found almost no support. His colleagues saw that other factors also needed consideration, among them that thousands of men were daily being killed on both sides, and that we would be guilty of permitting this slaughter to continue if we did not use what power we had to bring the war to a close. Accordingly he rephrased his petition so as to approve of the use of the atomic weapons after giving suitable warning and opportunity for surrender under known conditions. As he turned the revised petition over to me for delivery to Washington, Szilard indicated that it was signed by sixty-seven scientists residing in Chicago.

The reaction to this petition among members of the project was vigorous. One counterpetition read in part thus:

> Are not the men of the fighting forces a part of the nation? Are not they, who are risking their lives for the nation entitled to the weapons which have been designed? In short, are we to go on shedding American blood when we have available a means to speedy victory? No! If we can save even a handful of American lives, then let us use this weapon—now!
> . . . These sentiments, we feel, represent more truly those of the majority of Americans and particularly those who have sons . . . in the foxholes and warships in the Pacific.

One of the young men who had been with us at Chicago and had transferred to Los Alamos came into my Chicago office in a state of emotional stress. He said he had heard of an effort [**242/243**] to prevent the use of the bomb. Two years earlier I had persuaded this young man, as he was graduating with a major in physics, to cast his lot with our project. The chances are, I had told him, that you will be able to contribute more toward winning the war in this position than if you should accept the call to the Navy that you are considering. He had heeded my advice. Now he was sorely troubled: 'I have buddies who have fought through the battle of Iwo Jima. Some of them have been killed, others wounded. We've got to give these men the best weapons we can produce.' Tears came to his eyes. 'If one of these men should be killed because we didn't let them use the bombs, I would have failed them. I just could not make myself feel that I had done my part.' Others, though less emotional, felt just as deeply.

An especially carefully considered petition that carried a large number of signatures reads as if those who framed it had been reading the minds of Mr. Truman and Mr. Stimson. It was addressed to the President:

. . . We respectfully petition that the use of atomic bombs, particularly against cities, be sanctioned by you as Chief Executive only under the following conditions:

1. Opportunity has been given to the Japanese to surrender on terms assuring them the possibility of peaceful development in their homeland.

2. Convincing warnings have been given that refusal to surrender will be followed by the use of a new weapon.

3. Responsibility for the use of atomic bombs is shared with our allies.

It was difficult from such petitions to get a balanced view of how our men were thinking. General Groves accordingly suggested that I supervise an opinion poll among those who knew what was going on. Farrington Daniels, then Director of the Metallurgical Laboratory, took charge of the poll at Chicago. Oppenheimer at Los Alamos and Lawrence at Berkeley used [**243/244**] less formal methods of sounding the opinions of their men. It was attitudes thus expressed that the Scientific Panel had in mind as we wrote our report to the Interim Committee reluctantly rejecting the nonmilitary demonstration of the bomb.

Daniels asked and received replies from 150 members of the Metallurgical Laboratory at Chicago. His questionnaire had five procedures, graded from no use of the bomb in this war to its military use in the manner most effective in bringing prompt Japanese surrender. There were a few who preferred not to use the bomb at all, but 87 per cent voted for its military use, at least if after other means were tried this was found necessary to bring surrender.[9]

My experience with this questionnaire has confirmed my faith in the reliability of democratic processes in judging matters of human concern. It is a striking fact that the same points of view were presented with closely the same degree of relative frequency by men active in widely different areas. The three groups to which I refer were: (1) the men in the Interim Committee, individuals concerned with human problems in their broadest terms and accustomed to accepting the responsibility for major decisions; (2) the scientists and other scholars whose professional activities were primarily of an intellectual type; (3) the mechanics in our shops who were working long hours in fabricating the bomb or in building instruments concerned with its development. When it comes to questions of the value associated with human life, judgments are from the heart.

. . . .

[9] Daniels, Farrington, and Compton, A. H., 'A Poll of Scientists at Chicago,' *Bulletin of Atomic Scientists* 4 (February 1948) 44.

A Personal History of the Bomb*

LEO SZILARD (1898-1964), professor of physics, collaborated with Enrico Fermi in constructing an atomic pile at the University of Chicago in 1942, which paved the way for the development of the bomb three years later. In 1939 he persuaded Albert Einstein to write a letter to President Roosevelt recommending the development of atomic energy as a potential military weapon. However, he subsequently opposed use of the bomb against Japan. After the war Professor Szilard became a leading spokesman for atomic disarmament. In 1959 he received an Atoms for Peace award.

. . . .

During the war, while we worked on the bomb, we scientists thought for a while that we were in a neck-and-neck race with the Germans and that getting the bomb first might make the difference between winning or losing the war. But, when Germany was defeated, many of us became uneasy about the proposed use of the bomb in the war with Japan. Many of us were uneasy about how the existence of the bomb would affect the position of the United States after the war.

After President Roosevelt's death and six weeks before the bomb was tested in New Mexico, I tried to reach the White House and was directed to call upon Mr. Byrnes. There were three of us who went to see him, and H. C. Urey was one of us. Byrnes was not at that time Secretary of State, but he knew of the bomb and had given some thought to problems of foreign policy. The question of whether the bomb should be used in the war against Japan came up for discussion. Mr. Byrnes did not argue that it was necessary to use the bomb against the cities of Japan in order to win the war. He knew at that time, as the rest of the Government knew, that Japan was essentially defeated and that we could win the war in another six months. At that time Mr. Byrnes was much concerned about the spreading of Russian influence in Europe; Rumania, Bulgaria, Yugoslavia, Czechoslovakia, and Hungary were all living under a shadow cast by Russia. Mr. Byrnes's concern about Russia I fully shared, but his view that our possessing and demonstrating the bomb would [**14/15**] make Russia more manageable in Europe I was not able to share. Indeed I could hardly imagine any premise more false or disastrous upon which to base our policy, and I was dismayed when a few weeks later I learned that he was to be our Secretary of State.

On my return to Chicago, sixty-three of us scientists sent a petition to the President. We asked him not to set a precedent for the use of atomic energy for purposes of destruction by approving the military use of the bomb against the cities of Japan. Our attitude was by no means shared by all scientists. There was another group of scientists, centering on Los Alamos under the leadership of J.R. Oppenheimer, who had no objection to the use of the bomb against Japan but laid much emphasis on informing the Russians of our intentions before we

* Leo Szilard, from "A Personal History of the Bomb," *The University of Chicago Roundtable,* September 25, 1949, pp. 14-16. Reprinted by permission of the University of Chicago Press.

dropped the bomb. This view was fully shared by Secretary Stimson, who urged President Truman to inform Marshal Stalin at Potsdam of our plan to use the bomb.

Mr. Byrnes relates in his book, *Speaking Frankly,* how President Truman made an attempt at Potsdam to tell Stalin about the bomb. Stalin happened to be engrossed at that moment in discussing Russian transportation problems and double-track railroads. He did not show any particular interest when he was told that we had a very powerful new bomb which we proposed to use against Japan, and so President Truman dropped the matter. One could hardly say that the attempt to inform Stalin was a very vigorous one. Mr. Truman did not say, "Excuse me, Mr. Stalin, but you do not seem to understand. I am not speaking of just another bomb; I am speaking of something that will get Russia and the United States into the greatest difficulties after the war unless we find a solution to the problem which it poses." Mr. Truman said nothing of the sort. So the bomb was dropped on Hiroshima and caught the Russians by surprise. "We have gambled two billion dollars and won," said the President's statement announcing the bombing of Hiroshima.

. . . .

A Report to the Secretary of War, June 1945*

THE COMMITTEE OF SOCIAL AND POLITICAL IMPLICATIONS was appointed by the director of the Metallurgical Laboratory in Chicago. The committee was composed of three physicists (James Franck, D. Hughes, and Leo Szilard), three chemists (T. Hogness, E. Rabinowich and G. Seaborg), and one biologist (C. J. Nickson). Under the chairmanship of Dr. Franck the committee sent the following petition to Secretary of War Henry L. Stimson in June, 1945, six days before the test explosion in New Mexico. This petition, commonly called "The Franck Report," was the most formal statement protesting use of the atomic bomb as a military weapon.

I. PREAMBLE

The only reason to treat nuclear power differently from all the other developments in the field of physics is the possibility of its use as a means of political pressure in peace and sudden destruction in war. All present plans for the organization of research, scientific and industrial development, and publication in the field of nucleonics are conditioned by the political and military climate in which one expects those plans to be carried out. Therefore, in making suggestions for the postwar organization of nucleonics, a discussion of political problems cannot be avoided. The scientists on this Project do not presume to speak authoritatively on problems of national and international policy. However, we found ourselves, by the force of events, during the last five years, in the position of a small group of citizens cognizant of a grave danger for the safety of this country as well as for the future of all the other nations, of which the rest of mankind is unaware. We therefore feel it our duty to urge that the political problems, arising from the mastering of nuclear power, be recognized in all their gravity, and that appropriate steps be taken for their study and the preparation of necessary decisions. We hope that the creation of the Committee by the Secretary of War to deal with all aspects of nucleonics, indicates that these implications have been recognized by the government. We believe that our acquaintance with the scientific elements of the situation and prolonged preoccupation with its world-wide political implications, imposes on us the obligation to offer to the Committee some suggestions as to the possible solution of these grave problems.

* * *

Scientists have often before been accused of providing new weapons for the mutual destruction of nations, instead of improving their well-being. It is undoubtedly true that the discovery of flying, for example, has so far brought much more misery than enjoyment and profit to humanity. However, in the past, scientists could disclaim direct responsibility for the use to which mankind had put their disinterested discoveries. We feel compelled to take a more active stand now because the success which we have achieved in the development of nuclear power is

* The Committee of Social and Political Implications, from "A Report to the Secretary of War, June 1945," *Bulletin of the Atomic Scientists*, May 1, 1946, pp. 2-4, 16.

fraught with infinitely greater dangers than were all the inventions of the past. All of us, familiar with the present state of nucleonics, live with the vision before our eyes of sudden destruction visited on our own country, of a Pearl Harbor disaster repeated in thousand-fold magnification in every one of our major cities.

In the past, science has often been able to provide also new methods of protection against new weapons of aggression it made possible, but it cannot promise such efficient protection against the destructive use of nuclear power. This protection can come only from the political organization of the world. Among all the arguments calling for an efficient international organization for peace, the existence of nuclear weapons is the most compelling one. In the absence of an international authority which would make all resort to force in international conflicts impossible, nations could still be diverted from a path which must lead to total mutual destruction, by a specific international agreement barring a nuclear armaments race. [**2/3**]

. . . .

* * *

One possible way to introduce nuclear weapons to one world—which may particularly appeal to those who consider nuclear bombs primarily as a secret weapon developed to help win the present war—is to use them without warning on appropriately selected objects in Japan.

Although important tactical results undoubtedly can be achieved by a sudden introduction of nuclear weapons, we nevertheless think that the question of the use of the very first available atomic bombs in the Japanese war should be weighed very carefully, not only by military authorities, but by the highest political leadership of this country.

Russia, and even allied countries which bear less mistrust of our ways and intentions, as well as neutral countries may be deeply shocked by this step. It may be very difficult to persuade the world that a nation which was capable of secretly preparing and suddenly releasing a new weapon, as indiscriminate as the rocket bomb and a thousand times more destructive, is to be trusted in its proclaimed desire of having such weapons abolished by international agreement. We have large accumulations of poison gas, but do not use them, and recent polls have shown that public opinion in this country would disapprove of such a use even if it would accelerate the winning of the Far Eastern war. It is true that some irrational element in mass psychology makes gas poisoning more revolting than blasting by explosives, even though gas warfare is in no way more "inhuman" than the war of bombs and bullets. Nevertheless, it is not at all certain that American public opinion, if it could be enlightened as to the effect of atomic explosives, would approve of our own country being the first to introduce such an indiscriminate method of wholesale destruction of civilian life.

Thus, from the "optimistic" point of view—looking forward to an international agreement on the prevention of nuclear warfare—the military advantages and the saving of American lives achieved by the sudden use of atomic bombs against Japan may be outweighed by the ensuing loss of confidence and by a wave of horror and repulsion sweeping over the rest of the world and perhaps even dividing public opinion at home.

From this point of view, a demonstration of the new weapon might best be made, before the eyes of representatives of all the United Nations, on the desert or a barren island. The best possible atmosphere for the achievement of an international agreement could be achieved if America could say to the world, "You see what sort of a weapon we had but did not use. We are ready to renounce its use in the future if other nations join us in this renunciation and agree to the establishment of an efficient international control."

After such a demonstration the weapon might perhaps be used against Japan if the sanction of the United Nations (and of public opinion at home) were obtained, perhaps after a preliminary ultimatum to Japan to surrender or at least to evacuate certain regions as an alternative to their total destruction. This may sound fantastic, but in nuclear weapons we have something entirely new in order of magnitude of destructive power, and if we want [**3/4**] to capitalize fully on the advantage their possession gives us, we must use new and imaginative methods.

* * *

It must be stressed that if one takes the pessimistic point of view and discounts the possibility of an effective international control over nuclear weapons at the present time, then the advisability of an early use of nuclear bombs against Japan becomes even more doubtful—quite independently of any humanitarian considerations. If an international agreement is not concluded immediately after the first demonstration, this will mean a flying start toward an unlimited armaments race. If this race is inevitable, we have every reason to delay its beginning as long as possible in order to increase our head start still further.

* * *

The benefit to the nation, and the saving of American lives in the future, achieved by renouncing an early demonstration of nuclear bombs and letting the other nations come into the race only reluctantly, on the basis of guesswork and without definite knowledge that the "thing does work," may far outweigh the advantages to be gained by the immediate use of the first and comparatively inefficient bombs in the war against Japan. On the other hand, it may be argued that without an early demonstration it may prove difficult to obtain adequate support for further intensive development of nucleonics in this country and that thus the time gained by the postponements of an open armaments race will not be properly used. Furthermore one may suggest that other nations are now, or will soon be, not entirely unaware of our present achievements, and that consequently the postponement of a demonstration may serve no useful purpose as far as the avoidance of an armaments race is concerned, and may only create additional mistrust, thus worsening rather than improving the chances of an ultimate accord on the international control of nuclear explosives.

Thus, if the prospects of an agreement will be considered poor in the immediate future, the pros and cons of an early revelation of our possession of nuclear weapons to the world—not only by their actual use against Japan, but also by a prearranged demonstration—must be carefully weighed by the supreme political and military leadership of the country, and the decision should not be left to the considerations of military tactics alone.

One may point out that scientists themselves have initiated the development of this "secret weapon" and it is therefore strange that they should be reluctant to try it out on the enemy as soon as it is available. The answer to this question was given above—the compelling reason for creating this weapon with such speed was our fear that Germany had the technical skill necessary to develop such a weapon, and that the German government had no moral restraints regarding its use.

Another argument which could be quoted in favor of using atomic bombs as soon as they are available is that so much taxpayers' money has been invested in these Projects that the Congress and the American public will demand a return for their money. The attitude of American public opinion, mentioned earlier, in the matter of the use of poison gas against Japan, shows that one can expect the American public to understand that it is sometimes desirable to keep a weapon in readiness for use only in extreme emergency; and as soon as the potentialities of nuclear weapons are revealed to the American people, one can be sure that they will support all attempts to make the use of such weapons impossible.

Once this is achieved, the large installations and the accumulation of explosive material at present earmarked for potential military use will become available for important peace-time developments, including power production, large engineering undertakings, and mass production of radioactive materials. In this way, the money spent on wartime development of nucleonics may become a boon for the peacetime development of national economy.

. . . .

SUMMARY

The development of nuclear power not only constitutes an important addition to the technological and military power of the United States, but also creates grave political and economic problems for the future of this country.

Nuclear bombs cannot possibly remain a "secret weapon" at the exclusive disposal of this country for more than a few years. The scientific facts on which their construction is based are well known to scientists of other countries. Unless an effective international control of nuclear explosives is instituted, a race for nuclear armaments is certain to ensue following the first revelation of our possession of nuclear weapons to the world. Within ten years other countries may have nuclear bombs, each of which weighing less than a ton, could destroy an urban area of more than ten square miles. In the war to which such an armaments race is likely to lead, the United States, with its agglomeration [**4/16**] of population and industry in comparatively few metropolitan districts, will be at a disadvantage compared to nations whose population and industry are scattered over large areas.

We believe that these considerations make the use of nuclear bombs for an early unannounced attack against Japan inadvisable. If the United States were to be the first to release this new means of indiscriminate destruction upon mankind, she would sacrifice public support throughout the world, precipitate the race for armaments, and prejudice the possibility of reaching an international agreement on the future control of such weapons.

Much more favorable conditions for the eventual achievement of such an agreement could be created if nuclear bombs were first revealed to the world by a demonstration in an appropriately selected uninhabited area.

In case chances for the establishment of an effective international control of nuclear weapons should have to be considered slight at the present time, then not only the use of these weapons against Japan, but even their early demonstration, may be contrary to the interests of this country. A postponement of such a demonstration will have in this case the advantage of delaying the beginning of the nuclear armaments race as long as possible.

If the government should decide in favor of an early demonstration of nuclear weapons, it will then have the possibility of taking into account the public opinion of this country and of the other nations before deciding whether these weapons should be used against Japan. In this way, other nations may assume a share of responsibility for such a fateful decision.

The Fight Over the A-Bomb*

FLETCHER KNEBEL (1911-) and **CHARLES W. BAILEY** (1929-) are members of *Look* magazine's Washington bureau. Both men have been connected with a number of newspapers in different parts of the country, and, in addition to their association with *Look,* they are also on the Washington staff of the Minneapolis *Tribune.* Together they co-authored two books, *No High Ground* (1960), an account of the effort to develop the atomic bomb, and *Seven Days in May* (1962), a best-selling novel about a *coup d'etat* against the United States government. "The Fight Over the A-Bomb" was prepared on the basis of information contained in previously secret files of the wartime atomic energy project. Access to a limited portion of these files was granted to Knebel and Bailey in 1961, but their article was then denied clearance by the State Department. In June 1963, clearance was given.

When President Harry S. Truman ordered the dropping of the atomic bomb on Japan, in an effort to end World War II with one swift stroke, he touched off a debate that will endure as long as men survive to write history.

No serious student can question the motives or the integrity of the men who made that fateful decision. Behind them lay more than three years of bloody, bitter fighting. Yet one question has troubled those who study the issue: Were the men who actually unlocked the power of the atom—the nuclear scientists themselves—given a full hearing?

Now, from behind the security curtain surrounding the atomic project, comes an answer:

President Truman, faced with one of the great moral decisions of human history, was denied access to the petitions of many American nuclear scientists who opposed the dropping of the atomic bomb on Hiroshima without warning.

This startling fact emerges from the official files of the Manhattan Project, the $2 billion complex that built the bomb. Policy papers from these files, classified "Top Secret" for 18 years, were obtained by LOOK after a two-year security clearance process that involved the Defense Department, the State Department and the Atomic Energy Commission. [**19/20**]

. . . .

In essence, the first great moral debate of the atomic age was personified by two strong-minded men, one a refugee scientist, the other an Army general. Many others participated in the secret struggle, but these two became the symbols.

Against the bomb: Leo Szilard, a brilliant Hungarian physicist who had studied at the University of Berlin, but fled to the United States after the rise of Hitler. As much as any other man, he was responsible for persuading Franklin D. Roosevelt to undertake atomic-weapons research in the first place. With Enrico Fermi, he supervised the first controlled chain reaction in a squash court under the football stands of Stagg Field at the University of Chicago.

For the bomb: Maj Gen. Leslie Richard Groves, a West Point-educated Army engineer who built the Pentagon and then took over the prodigious "Manhattan Engineer District" to build the atomic bomb. A big man, handsome and fearless, he literally drove a vast army of scientists, factory workers and military officers to accomplish a feat that changed the world forever.

Both men still live today, and the fervor of their differences continues unabated. Szilard, at 65, and Groves, at 66, still cling to the views that cleaved them 18 years ago. Groves still believes the decision to use the bomb was right. Szilard still believes it was wrong.

Here are highlights of the epic dispute, in which Szilard and Groves stood at opposite poles, as revealed in the Manhattan papers:

- A bundle of scientific petitions and statements, largely opposed to unrestricted use of the A-bomb on Japan, never reached President Truman—although they were addressed to him, and Col. Kenneth D. Nichols, production chief of Manhattan, had urged Groves "that these papers be forwarded to the President of the United States with proper comments."
- America's top military officer of World War II, Gen. George C. Marshall, urged that the A-bomb should not be used against Japan except after adequate warning. Said Marshall: "We must offset by such warning methods the opprobrium which might follow from an ill-considered employment of such force." His advice was not followed.
- Apparently, only few opposition statements ever reached Truman. One was a passionate letter from O. C. Brewster of New York, who was involved in atomic production, and who wrote the President: "This thing must not be permitted to exist on earth." Another was the official dissent of Ralph A. Bard, the Under Secretary of the Navy, who argued that the Japanese should be warned that atomic power might be used.
- As early as September 30, 1944, many months before the first atomic device was tested and before Manhattan officials were even sure it would work, two distinguished Americans, James B. Conant, president of Harvard University, and Vannevar Bush, president of the Carnegie Institution of Washington, warned Secretary of War Henry L. Stimson of future "super-super" bombs that could be delivered by guided missiles. They urged that America demonstrate its first bomb for the Japanese before actually using it against Japan.
- The Interim Committee, set up at Stimson's suggestion in the spring of 1945 to study all implications of the atomic bomb, started with the assumption that the bomb would be used and never really weighed the opinions of the opposing scientists.
- Almost all American leaders privy to the atomic secret—military, scientific and political—were concerned about possible Russian duplicity and were extremely wary about informing Russia, our World War II ally, of our atomic progress. This was one of the few areas of general agreement in the otherwise divisive dispute over use of the bomb on Japan.
- Nowhere in the Manhattan papers is there any indication that President Truman ever made an affirmative decision to drop the bomb. Rather, he seems to have proceeded on the assumption that the bomb would be dropped when ready. The papers tend to confirm a recent statement by Groves that Truman "was like a little boy on a toboggan," who never had an opportunity to say yes. All he could have said, Groves argued, was no. That word the President never uttered. [**20/22**]

. . . .

On July 25, the day Secretary Stimson approved final orders to drop an A-bomb on Japan without warning "after about 3 August 1945," Colonel Nichols at the Oak Ridge, Tenn., atomic site bundled up a batch of letters and petitions and sent them by Manhattan security messenger to General Groves in Washington.

Most important was a sealed brown manila envelope marked "P. O. Box 5207, Chicago 80, Illinois," and addressed in ink "To The President Of The United States." This was Szilard's appeal to Truman, buttressed by the signatures of such prominent atomic scientists as Ralph E. Lapp, Eugene P. Wigner and Walter Bartky.

Szilard and his colleagues urged Truman not to use the bomb "unless the terms which will be imposed upon Japan have been made public in detail and Japan, knowing these terms, has refused to surrender; second, that in such an event the question whether or not to use atomic bombs be decided by you in the light of the considerations presented in this petition as well as all the other moral responsibilities which are involved."

This was compromise language, for Szilard's first draft, written July 3, would have asked Truman not to use the bomb at all. When this original petition began circulating at the Chicago laboratory, Grover C. Thompson, a security officer, reported it to Groves. The General said it was all right to let the petition circulate, provided it went through security channels and was not shown to scientists who had less information about the bomb than Szilard. Szilard's first-draft plea to the President concluded:

"We, the undersigned, respectfully petition that you exercise your power as commander-in-chief to rule that the United States shall not, in the present phase of the war, resort to the use of atomic bombs."

Szilard modified his petition—changing it from a plea for no use of the A-bomb at all to a plea for use only after warning to Japan—after discussing the issue with a number of his colleagues. As revised, it drew 70 signatures.

Another enclosure in the package for Groves was a document signed by 68 scientists at Oak Ridge, recommending that "before the weapon be used without restriction in the present conflict, its powers should be adequately described and demonstrated, and the Japanese nation should be given the opportunity to consider the consequences of further refusal to surrender."

Still another was signed by 18 Chicago scientists. They agreed generally with Szilard, but said their feeling was more explicitly expressed in these words:

"We respectfully petition that the use of atomic bombs, particularly against cities, be sanctioned by you as Chief Executive only under the following conditions:

"1. Opportunity has been given the Japanese to surrender on terms assuring them the possibility of peaceful development in their homeland.

"2. Convincing warnings have been given that a refusal to surrender will be followed by use of a new weapon.

"3. Responsibility for use of atomic bombs is shared with our allies."

Also included in the package was a poll of 150 scientists at Chicago who were asked by Farrington Daniels, director of the laboratory, to choose among five possible courses. By far the largest number, 46 percent, voted to "give a military demonstration in Japan, to be followed by a renewed opportunity to surrender before full use of the weapon is employed."

In a letter forwarded with the poll, Arthur Compton pointed out **[22/23]** that this option was "the strongly favored procedure."

"This coincides," said Compton, "with my own preference and is, as nearly as I can judge, the procedure that has found most favor in all informed groups where the subject has been discussed."

The phrase "military demonstration in Japan" was promptly interpreted by pro-bomb officials as meaning an attack without warning, though many of the poll participants later contended they meant just the opposite, and that the phrase "before full use of the weapon is employed" clearly implied that they first wanted an atomic demonstration that would not kill large masses of people.

Two of the letters in the bundle were "pro-bomb." One was from Evan J. Young, a chemist at Oak Ridge, noting the objections of his fellow scientists, but stating that incendiary bombing raids on Japan had already inflicted a "fiendish hell" on that country.

The second was from George W. Parker, another atomic chemist working at Oak Ridge. He argued for the "greatest strategic use of the weapon for the smallest loss of American life and the most conclusive victory over Japan."

In forwarding the bundle to Groves, Colonel Nichols added a covering letter of his own. He said that "contrary to the hopes of Mr. Leo Szilard . . . it is believed that these collective papers generally support the present plans for use of the weapons." Nichols urged, on July 25, that "these papers be forwarded to the President of the United States with proper comments."

But President Truman never saw them. He was then in Potsdam at the conference with Stalin and the British. Groves, according to the evidence in the Manhattan files, held the bundle of petitions until August 1, when a messenger delivered them to Stimson's office. Truman was about to embark for home aboard the U.S.S. *Augusta*. The bomb was dropped on Hiroshima on August 6, while Truman was still aboard the warship in the Atlantic.

Almost a year later, on May 24, 1946, Arneson wrote a memorandum for the Interim Committee files explaining what happened. He said that since the question of the bomb's use "had already been fully considered and settled by the proper authorities," and since scientists had been given adequate opportunity to present their views to the Interim Committee "through the scientific panel," it was decided that "no useful purpose would be served by transmitting either the petition or any of the attached documents to the White House, particularly since the President was not then in the country."

General Marshall's reservations on use of the bomb, which remained unknown until the unlocking of the Manhattan papers, were disclosed to Stimson and Assistant Secretary of War John J. McCloy at a meeting in Stimson's office on May 29, 1945. McCloy made a memorandum of the discussion, and Marshall approved it as written. The memo records that Marshall stressed the need of warning the Japanese, a course that was not followed before the drop on Hiroshima.

"General Marshall," noted McCloy, "said he thought these weapons might first be used against straight military objectives such as a large naval installation, and then if no complete result was derived from the effect of that, he thought we ought to designate a number of large manufacturing areas from which people would be warned to leave—telling the Japanese that we intended to destroy such centers. There would be no individual designations so that the Japs would not know exactly where we were to hit—a number should be named and the hit should follow shortly after.

"Every effort should be made to keep our record of warning clear. We must offset by such warning methods the opprobrium which might follow from an ill-considered employment of such force."

Marshall went on to say that he was considering the "limited" use of a nonlethal poison gas against "fanatical but hopeless" Japanese pockets of resistance. Marshall said the gas would not kill, but would permit quick cleanup of suicidal defenders. He realized that public opinion might not support the use of gas. but said it was no less humane than "phosphorus and flamethrowers."

. . . .

The day the first atomic bomb wiped out Hiroshima, without warning and without a prior demonstration, Leo Szilard asked permission to make public his petition to President Truman—the petition that had asked the President not to use the bomb until the moral issue had been resolved.

On August 9, the same day that the

second atomic bomb fell on Nagasaki, Szilard got his answer in the form of a message from one of Groves's security officers: Request disapproved. Groves was still pushing his vast machine hard. The next day, he notified General Marshall that four days had been gained in the assembly of a third bomb, and that it would be ready to drop on Japan by August 17 or 18.

The Japanese surrendered on August 14, and the third bomb was never dropped. The lid of peacetime official secrecy snapped shut on the files of the Manhattan Project.

It was not until the opening of the files, 18 years later, that Leo Szilard could learn that President Truman never saw his petition—nor those of Szilard's colleagues—before an atomic bomb, in a fraction of a second over Hiroshima, changed the course of history.

PART THREE
THE JAPANESE REACTION

*The Cause of Japan**

SHIGENORI TOGO (1882-1950) was foreign minister of Japan at the time of Pearl Harbor and also at the end of the war. His diplomatic career included appointments as ambassador to Germany (1937) and to Moscow (1938-1941). Togo was identified with the anti-militarist faction in the Japanese government, and he was recalled from retirement in April, 1945, to participate in the cabinet formed by Admiral Suzuki which arranged the surrender. After the war he was convicted of war crimes; he later died in an American military hospital.

. . . .

Already, from before this time [June, 1945], the United States had frequently broadcast reports that Japan would sue for unconditional surrender. Japan, however, was in no state to surrender unconditionally—indeed, Japan maintained up to the end, up to the ultimate acceptance of the Potsdam Declaration, the position that she accepted the declaration unconditionally, but that that was not to surrender unconditionally. The unconditional surrender applied to the armed forces only (as was clearly stated in the declaration itself), not to the nation. This American propaganda and insistence on "unconditional surrender," therefore, hampered to no small extent the progress of the movement in Japan for peace. [**299/300**]

. . . .

By late June the war in every aspect had become critical. Production decreased drastically, on account of the air attacks and the breakdown of transportation facilities—not only did the production of aircraft dwindle, but even (for example) salt, essential to the manufacture of explosives, became scarce. The food shortage grew acute, and serious unrest of the populace by winter could be predicted. It seemed that informed quarters everywhere, official and private alike, were realizing the impossibility of going on with the struggle, and from every side the pressure to make peace mounted. Agriculture and Forestry Minister Ishiguro and Minister without Portfolio Sakonji called on me specially to confide their fears, as did other ministers. The feeling of non-official circles was expressed by Professors Nambara and Takagi of Tokyo Imperial University, who came to urge upon me the speedy achieving of peace—I told them that the moves which I was making were in exact conformity with their object, and added that I would appreciate it if Professor Takagi, an expert on American affairs, could suggest any plan by which [**300/301**] to make direct contact with some quarter in the United States in order to try to bring about a negotiated peace. The politicians joined in, including even a Socialist Diet member who wanted me, despite the traditional bad relations between the Second and Third Internationals, to arrange for him to go to Moscow to get in touch with the United States. I found it strange that from former officials of the Foreign Minis-

* Shigenori Togo, from *The Cause of Japan* (New York: Simon and Schuster, Inc., 1956), pp. 299-301, 309-322.

try only had I no comunications concerning the necessity of ending the war. [**301/309**]

. . . .

During the early morning of 26 July, the day after Prime Minister Churchill's return to London for announcement of the result of the British general election, a joint declaration in the names of President Truman, Churchill and Generalissimo Chiang Kai-shek was issued at Potsdam. The text of this "Potsdam Declaration" is as follows.

1. We—the President of the United States, the President of the National Government of the Republic of China, and the Prime Minister of Great Britain, representing the hundreds of millions of our countrymen, have conferred and agree that Japan shall be given an opportunity to end this war.

2. The prodigious land, sea and air forces of the United States, the British Empire and of China, many times reinforced by their armies and air fleets from the west, are poised to strike the final blows upon Japan. This military power is sustained and inspired by the determination of all the Allied Nations to prosecute the war against Japan until she ceases to resist.

3. The result of the futile and senseless German resistance to the might of the aroused free peoples of the world stands forth in awful clarity as an example to the people of Japan. The might that now converges on Japan is immeasurably greater than that which, when applied to the resisting Nazis, necessarily laid waste to the lands, the industry and the method of life of the whole German people. The full application of our military [**309/310**] power, backed by our resolve, will mean the inevitable and complete destruction of the Japanese armed forces and just as inevitably the utter devastation of the Japanese homeland.

4. The time has come for Japan to decide whether she will continue to be controlled by those self-willed militaristic advisers whose unintelligent calculations have brought the Empire of Japan to the threshold of annihilation, or whether she will follow the path of reason.

5. Following are our terms. We will not deviate from them. There are no alternatives. We shall brook no delay.

6. There must be eliminated for all time the authority and influence of those who have deceived and misled the people of Japan into embarking on world conquest, for we insist that a new order of peace, security and justice will be impossible until irresponsible militarism is driven from the world.

7. Until such a new order is established and there is convincing proof that Japan's war-making power is destroyed, points in Japanese territory to be designated by the Allies shall be occupied to secure the achievement of the basic objectives we are here setting forth.

8. The terms of the Cairo Declaration shall be carried out and Japanese sovereignty shall be limited to the islands of Honshu, Hokkaido, Kyushu, Shikoku and such minor islands as we determine.

9. The Japanese military forces, after being completely disarmed, shall be permitted to return to their homes with the opportunity to lead peaceful and productive lives.

10. We do not intend that the Japanese shall be enslaved as a race or destroyed as a nation, but stern justice shall be meted out to all war criminals, including those who have visited cruelties upon our prisoners. The Japanese Government shall remove all obstacles to the revival and strengthening of democratic tendencies among the Japanese people. Freedom of speech, of religion, and of thought, as well as respect for the fundamental human rights, shall be established.

11. Japan shall be permitted to maintain such industries as will sustain her economy and permit the exaction of just reparations in kind, but not those which would enable her to re-arm for war. To this end, access to, as distinguished from control of, raw materials shall be permitted. Eventual Japanese participation in world trade relations shall be permitted. [**310/311**]

12. The occupying forces of the Allies shall be withdrawn from Japan as soon as these objectives have been accomplished and there has been established in accordance with the freely expressed will of the Japanese people a peacefully inclined and responsible government.

13. We call upon the government of Japan to proclaim now the unconditional surrender of all Japanese armed forces, and to provide proper and adequate assurances of their good faith in such action. The alternative for Japan is prompt and utter destruction.

My first reaction to the declaration upon reading through the text as broadcast by the American radio was that, in view of the language, "Following are our terms," it was evidently not a dictate of unconditional surrender. I got the impression that the Emperor's wishes had reached the United States and Great Britain, and had had the result of this moderation of their attitude. It appeared also that a measure of consideration had been given to Japan's economic position;

at a time when such Draconian retribution upon Germany as the "Morgenthau Plan" for her reduction to a "pastoral state" was being proposed, I felt special relief upon seeing the economic provisions of the declaration—the gist of them being that the function of Japan as a processing nation, as contemplated by Secretary Hull during the Japanese-American negotiations, would be recognized, and that to this end severe reparations would not be imposed.

The territorial provisions of the declaration I did not deem in the light of the Atlantic Charter to be fitting, for—putting aside the question of the independence of Korea—Formosa and our other territories would have to be surrendered in conformity with the edict of the Cairo Declaration, and our sovereignty would in effect be limited to the four main islands of Japan. As to the occupation, also, there were some doubts. The occupation seemed, it is true, to have applicability to designated points in our country, and it apparently was to be—unlike the treatment [**311/312**] of Germany after her surrender—a guarantee occupation not involving extensive administration; there was a question, however, whether Tokyo and the other large cities would be included among the points designated. I considered, further, that there were some ambiguities concerning the eventual form of the Japanese government, and also that complications might result from the language relating to disarmament and war criminals. I therefore instructed Foreign Vice-Minister Matsumoto[1] to make a careful study of the legal aspects of the declaration.

Simultaneously, I thought it desirable to enter into negotiation with the Allied Powers to obtain some clarification, and revision—even if it should be slight—of disadvantageous points in the declaration.

[1] Matsumoto Shun-ichi (1897-), a career diplomat, was Ambassador to Indochina, 1944-45, and Vice-Minister from May to September 1945. He was Ambassador to Great Britain, 1952-55, and since 1955 has been special envoy to negotiate, in London, a treaty of peace with the U.S.S.R.

I was received in audience on the morning of the 27th, and reported to the Emperor on recent happenings, including the negotiations with Moscow, the British general election and the Potsdam Declaration. I stressed that the declaration must be treated with the utmost circumspection, both domestically and internationally; in particular, I feared the consequences if Japan should manifest an intention to reject it. I pointed out further that the efforts to obtain Soviet mediation to bring about the ending of the war had not yet borne fruit, and that our attitude toward the declaration should be decided in accordance with their outcome.

At a meeting of the members of the Supreme Council for Direction of the War, held on the same day, I spoke to the same effect. On this occasion, Chief of Staff Toyoda said that news of the declaration would, sooner or later, transpire, and if we did [**312/313**] nothing it would lead to a serious impairment of morale; hence, he suggested, it would be best at this time to issue a statement that the government regarded the declaration as absurd and could not consider it. Premier Suzuki and I objected to this, and as a result it was agreed that for the time being we should wait to see what the response of the U.S.S.R. would be to our approach to her, planning to decide our course thereafter. On the same afternoon there was a Cabinet meeting, at which I reported on the negotiations with the U.S.S.R. which Mr. Hirota had been conducting, and on recent international developments in general. I went into detail concerning the Potsdam Declaration, and recommended that we should act on it after having ascertained the attitude of the Soviet Union. No dissent from this treatment of the declaration was expressed, though there was considerable discussion of the way and the extent of making it public. In the end it was agreed that it should be passed without comment by the government, the competent authorities releasing it in summary, while the Board of Information should lead the press to minimize publicity.

To my amazement, the newspapers of the following morning reported that the government had decided to ignore the Potsdam Declaration. I protested without delay to the Cabinet when it met, pointing out that the report was at variance with our decision of the preceding day. What had happened, I learned, was this. There had been held in the Imperial Palace, after adjournment of the Cabinet the day before, a conference for exchange of information between government and high command. This was a routine weekly meeting without special significance, and I had been absent because of more important business. One of the military participants in that meeting, as I heard it, had proposed the rejection of the Potsdam Declaration; the Premier, the [**313/314**] War and Navy Ministers and the two Chiefs of Staff had hastily assembled for consultation in a separate room, and the Premier had been persuaded by the more militant elements to that course. He then stated at a subsequent press conference that the government had decided to ignore the declaration, and this announcement it was which the press had played up so sensationally. It was only after the affair had developed to this point that I first knew of it; despite my thorough dissatisfaction with the position, there was of course no way of withdrawing the statement released by the Premier, and things had to be left as they stood. In the result, the American press reported that Japan had rejected the declaration, and President Truman in deciding for use of the atomic bomb, and the U.S.S.R. in attacking Japan, referred to the rejection of it as justification for their respective actions. The incident was thus a deplorable one in its embarrassment of our move for peace, and was most disadvantageous for Japan.

Meanwhile, despite my repeated instructions to Ambassador Satō in Moscow to press the U.S.S.R. to act quickly on our request for mediation, he did not succeed in obtaining access to any of the Russian officials save Vice-Commissar Lozovsky, until finally he reported that Molotov was back in Moscow from Potsdam on 5 August, and would receive him at 5:00 P.M. (11:00 P.M., Japan time) on the 8th. That interview proved, however—as we learned only after the war—to have no relation to our request, but to be for the quite different purpose of notifying the Ambassador of the U.S.S.R.'s commencement of war against Japan.

At 8:15 A.M. on 6 August the United States Air Force released over Hiroshima the atomic bomb the detonation of which was to reverberate down through the history of the world. I was informed that the damage was vast. I immediately demanded of [**314/315**] the Army the particulars; the American radio had announced that the bomb was one employing atomic fission, and if such a singular explosive had in fact been used, in violation of the international law of warfare, it would be necesary to lodge a protest with the United States. The Army replied to my inquiry that it could as yet say only that the bomb dropped on Hiroshima was one of high effectiveness, and that the details were under investigation. The United States and Great Britain launched large-scale propaganda on the atomic bomb, declaring that its use would alter utterly the character of war and would work a revolution in the life of the human race, and that if Japan did not accept the declaration of the three Powers the bomb would continue to be used until the nation was annihilated.

At a meeting of the Cabinet on the afternoon of 7 August the War and Home Ministers made reports on the Hiroshima bombing. The Army, pleading the necessity of awaiting the results of the investigation which had been ordered, obviously intended not to admit the nature of the atomic atack, but to minimize the effect of the bombing. On the 8th I had an audience, in the underground shelter of the Imperial Palace, with the Emperor, whom I informed of the enemy's announcement of the use of an atomic bomb, and related matters, and I said that it was now all the more imperative that we end the war, which we could seize this opportunity to do. The Emperor approved of my view, and warned that since we could no longer continue the struggle, now that a weapon of this devastating power was used against us, we should not let slip the opportunity by engaging in attempts to gain more favorable conditions. Since bargaining for terms had little prospect of success at this stage, he said, measures should be concerted to insure a prompt ending of hostilities. He further added that I should communicate his wishes to the Pre- [**315/316**] mier. Withdrawing, I spoke to Lord Keeper Kido of what had passed at my audience, and I then proceeded to inform the Premier at once of the Emperor's wishes and to request him to call a meeting of the members of the Supreme Council for Direction of the War.

In the early hours of the 9th the radio room of the Foreign Ministry telephoned to inform me of the U.S.S.R.'s broadcast of her declaration of war on us and the large-scale invasion of Manchuria by her forces. (Ambassador Satō, when he met with Commissar Molotov at 11:00 P.M., our time, on the 8th, had been notified of the declaration of war; but the cable report of the interview—and consequently of the declaration—which the Russians had assured him would be cleared for dispatch never reached Tokyo.) I visited the Premier early in the morning and told him of the Russian attack. Again I pointed out that the war must stop immediately, and Admiral Suzuki agreed. It was arranged that Chief Cabinet Secretary Sakomizu, who was present, should summon the members of the Supreme Council to an urgent conference. On the way to the Foreign Ministry I called at the Navy Ministry, and reported to Admiral Yonai as I had done to the Premier. While at the Navy Ministry I encountered Prince Takamatsu,[2] to whom also I explained why we must accept the Potsdam Declaration without further procrastination.

The members of the Supreme Council met at 11:00 A.M. I opened the discussion by saying that the war had become more and more hopeless, and now that it had no future, it was necessary to make peace without the slightest delay. Therefore, I said, the Potsdam Declaration must be complied with, and the conditions for its acceptance should be limited to those only which [**316/317**] were absolutely essential for Japan. All members of the Supreme Council already recognized the difficulties in going on with the war; and now, after the employment of the atomic bomb and Russian entry into the war against us, none opposed in principle our acceptance of the declaration. None disagreed, either, that we must insist upon preservation of the national polity as the indispensable condition of acceptance.

The military representatives, however, held out for proposing additional terms —specifically, that occupation of Japan should if possible be avoided or, if inescapable, should be on a small scale and should not include such points as Tokyo; that disarmament should be carried out on our responsibility; and that war criminals should be dealt with by Japan. I objected that in view of the recent attitude of Britain, America, Russia and China it was greatly to be feared that any proposal by us of a number of terms would be rejected, and that the entire effort for peace would be in danger of failing. Unless, therefore, the military services saw a prospect of winning the war, any terms proposed by us should be limited to the minimum of those truly vital; thus, while it was in order to propose other points as our desire, the only condition as such which we should hold out for was that of inviolability of the Imperial house. I asked, then, whether the armed services could offer any hope of victory in case

[2] Prince Takamatsu (1905-), the Emperor's second brother, was a rear admiral then on duty with the Naval General Staff.

negotiations on terms should be undertaken and should fail.

The War Minister replied that although he could give no assurance of ultimate victory, Japan could still fight another battle. I pressed them to say whether they could be certain of preventing the enemy from landing on our mainland. The Army Chief of Staff answered that we might drive the enemy into the sea if all went very well—though, in war, we could not be confident that things would go well—but that even conceding that a certain **[317/318]** percentage of the enemy's troops might succeed in establishing beachheads, he was confident that we could inflict heavy losses on them. I argued that this would be of no avail: according to the explanation given us by the Army, some part at least of the attackers might still land even after sustaining serious losses; but while it was obvious that the enemy would follow up with a second assault though the first was inadequately rewarded, we should have sacrificed most of our remaining aircraft and other important munitions in our efforts to destroy the first wave. There being no possibility of replenishing our supply of armaments in a short period, our position after the first enemy landing operations would be one of defenselessness, even leaving the atomic bomb out of account. My conclusion was that we had no alternative to stopping the war at this very moment, and we must therefore attempt to attain peace by limiting our counterdemands to the irreducible minimum.

The discussion became rather impassioned, but remained inconclusive, and it neared one o'clock, with a Cabinet meeting scheduled for the afternoon. The Premier stated that the question had to be submitted to the Cabinet also, and the Supreme Council adjourned without having come to any agreement how we should proceed.

The Cabinet met at two. Prior to the meeting, I said to Premier Suzuki that the Cabinet also was unlikely to arrive at a unanimous conclusion, in which event the only possible solution would be to request an Imperial decision; but it was necessary that the Premier take care lest the Cabinet be disabled, before that could be done—by the resignation of the War Minister, for instance. Also before the Cabinet meeting Vice-Minister Matsumoto came to me and said that the prevailing opinion of the Foreign Ministry likewise was that we should not present numerous conditions. **[318/319]**

At the Cabinet, I again detailed the course of the negotiations with the U.S.S.R., the use of the atomic bomb and the Soviet attack on us. There was the same controversy—whether we should accept the Potsdam Declaration with the one indispensable condition only, or should add the others, as proposed by the War Minister, relating to occupation, disarmament and war criminals. The Navy Minister sided with me, saying that there were no expectations to be indulged if we went on with the war; the War Minister opposed on the ground that if it came to a final battle on Japanese soil we could at least for a time repulse the enemy, and might thereafter somehow "find life out of death," even though there was no certainty of victory. In rebuttal I observed that according to the opinion of the high command as made known at the meeting of the council members, the prospects of driving the enemy into the sea were by no means bright, while even if we managed to punish them severely during their landings, our relative position would be far worse in the sequel. Discussion reached no issue. The meeting had gone on for hours, and it was now late at night. The Premier asked the Cabinet members to state their conclusions; some equivocated, some agreed with the Army's view, but most supported me.

At that point the Premier stated that he wished to report to the Emperor with me alone. Leaving the Cabinet in session, we went together to the Palace. Upon our being received, the Premier requested that I outline to the Emperor the disagreement in the Supreme Council and the Cabinet, which I did fully. The Premier then asked the Emperor's sanction for calling at once, that night, a meeting in his presence of the Supreme Council for Direction of the War. The Emperor approved, and the Imperial Conference convened shortly before midnight of the 9th. It was a full meeting; in addition to the Premier, the service ministers, **[319/320]** the two Chiefs of Staff and myself, Baron Hiranuma, President of the Privy Council, attended as a participant, and as secretaries there were the Chief Cabinet Secretary, the Director of the Combined Planning Bureau, General Ikeda, Director Yoshizumi of the War Ministry Military Affairs Bureau and Director Hoshina of the Navy Ministry Naval Affairs Bureau.

The Premier opened the conference by saying that, the deliberations at that morning's Supreme Council having failed to result in agreement on the accepting of the Potsdam Declaration, he wished to ask the Emperor to hear personally the opposing views. Thereupon two alternatives were submitted for consideration; one, to accept the Potsdam Declaration with the understanding that it comprised no demand which would prejudice the traditionally established status of the Emperor; the other, to attach in addition the three conditions before mentioned as insisted upon by the Army. I dilated upon the same points which I had argued at the Supreme Council members' meeting and that of the Cabinet, and contended that we must now end the war by accepting the Potsdam Declaration in accordance with the first alternative. The Navy Minister said simply that he fully concurred in the opinion of the Foreign Minister. But War Minister Anami reiterated his argument that we should propose the additional conditions, and the Army Chief of Staff anounced a similar conviction. Baron Hiranuma, after having asked a number of questions, called for amendment of the reservation in the first alternative to provide that the declaration "comprised no demand which would prejudice the prerogatives of the Emperor as a sovereign ruler"; this amendment being approved by all, Hiranuma agreed to that alternative.

There being still a division of opinion, the Premier said that he regretted that he must humbly beg the Emperor's decision. **[320/321]** The Emperor quietly said that he approved the opinion of the Foreign Minister; the confidence of the services in ultimate victory, he said, could not be relied upon, their earlier forecasts having often been at variance with the realities. As to the prospects of resisting invasion, even yet, he pointed out, the defenses of Kujūkurihama[3]—for example—were far from completion. Now, bearing the unbearable, he would submit to the terms of the Potsdam Declaration, thereby to preserve the national polity.

The Imperial Conference thereupon ended, at about half-past two. The Cabinet met at 3:00 A.M., and unanimously adopted a decision in conformity with the Emperor's words.

I hastened to the Foreign Ministry and drafted the telegram of notification to the Allies on the basis of the Imperial Conference decision. Communication to the United States having to go through the government of Switzerland, the Power protecting our interests, the message which follows was dispatched to Minister Kase in Bern at 7:00 A.M. of the 10th. An identical note went to Minister Okamoto in Stockholm for communication through the Swedish government to Great Britain and the U.S.S.R., and steps were taken to have our decision conveyed to the Chinese government also, through Switzerland.

In obedience to the gracious command of His Majesty the Emperor who, ever anxious to enhance the cause of world peace, desires earnestly to bring about a speedy termination of hostilities with a view to saving mankind from the calamities to be imposed upon them by further continuation of the war, the Japanese Government

[3] "Ninety-Nine-League Beach," on the Pacific seventy miles east of Tokyo. The Army had promised and had reported to the Emperor that the beach, expected to be a point of invasion, would be newly fortified and garrisoned by June.

several weeks ago asked the Soviet Government, with which neutral relations then prevailed, to render good offices in restoring peace vis-à-vis the enemy powers. Unfortunately, these efforts in the interest of peace having failed, the Japanese [321/322] Government in conformity with the august wish of His Majesty to restore the general peace and desiring to put an end to the untold sufferings entailed by war as quickly as possible, have decided upon the following.

The Japanese Government are ready to accept the terms enumerated in the joint declaration which was issued at Potsdam on July 26th, 1945, by the heads of the Governments of the United States, Great Britain, and China, and later subscribed by the Soviet Government, with the understanding that the said declaration does not comprise any demand which prejudices the prerogatives of His Majesty as a Sovereign Ruler.

The Japanese Government sincerely hope that this understanding is warranted and desire keenly that an explicit indication to that effect will be speedily forthcoming.

August 10, the 20th year of Shōwa.

. . . .

Invitation to Surrender*

TOSHIKAZU KASE (1903-   ) is a diplomat with wide experience in the Japanese Foreign Office. As a foreign service officer he was stationed in the United States, Germany, Thailand, and the United Kingdom. He served also as director of the Foreign Office's Information Bureau. When Japan surrendered, Mr. Kase became secretary to Foreign Minister Mamoru Shigemitsu. After temporary retirement he was recalled as a Foreign Office adviser when Shigemitsu was reappointed as foreign minister in 1954. From 1955 to 1957 he served as Japanese ambassador to the United Nations General Assembly. *Journey to the Missouri* (1950) contains an account of the events in Japan leading up to the surrender.

When the atomic bomb was dropped on Hiroshima on August 6 we could not make out at first what it actually was. The next day the San Francisco broadcast carried an announcement by President Truman that it was the atomic bomb. We were staggered. If a single bomb was equal in destructive power to the mass raid of a fleet of two thousand B-29's, with this lethal weapon the Allies could exterminate all life in Japan in less than a week! Further continuation of the war was mass suicide. Togo immediately went to the palace. The Emperor, showing deep concern over the fate of the helpless victims, said that since it was obviously impossible to defend the homeland any longer we had better conclude peace immediately without wasting time arguing about terms. That was common sense. But the Army, as ever, was a stranger to common sense. We tried to convince the thoughtless officers, saying that the appearance of the atomic bomb had revolutionized warfare. In spite of their avowed determination it was impossible with our inferior weapons to ward off the atomic attack. We even tried to save their face by advancing the plausible argument that it was not their fault if they laid down their arms; it was necessitated by the deplorable backwardness of our scientific research, which lagged far behind that of the United States and Great Britain.

However, the Army would not listen to reason. They were, as ever, riding on a hot steed headlong to self-destruction. They still defied the deepest powers of Hell. They even went to the length of forbidding the press to mention the atomic bomb lest it affect the people's morale. On August 7 GHQ issued the following communiqué:

> 1. In the attack made by a small number of B-29's on August 6 considerable damage was caused to Hiroshima city.
> 2. In this attack the enemy used a new type of bomb. Details are now under investigation.
>
> The new type bombs that were used by the superforts that raided Hiroshima on Monday morning were dropped by parachute and exploded before reaching the ground. A considerable number of houses in the city collapsed. The explosive power of the bomb is now under investigation, but it is considered that it should not be made light of. **[212/213]**

So for some time the press referred to the atomic bomb as merely "a new type

* Toshikasu Kase, from "Invitation to Surrender," *Journey to the Missouri* (New Haven: Yale University Press, 1950), pp. 212-218. Reprinted with the permission of Yale University Press.

of bomb"—while all the world was agog at the new terror. But the nation could not for long be left in ignorance, as the enemy radio widely disseminated the news. There were only three buildings left in all Hiroshima, a city which had never been bombed before. There was mile on mile of destruction and débris, range on range of collapsed city blocks where every building had been buffeted down and burned. The dead rotted away by the thousands, while mortally injured people, young as well as old, were left unattended to their fate amid the ruins.[17] "Naked trees and canted telephone poles; the few standing, gutted buildings only accentuating the horizontality of everything else . . . ; and in the streets a macabre traffic—hundreds of crumpled bicycles, shells of street cars and automobiles, all halted in mid-motion."[18] Such, indeed, was the ghastly aspect of the once prosperous city. This was more than the "considerable damage" reported in the GHQ communiqué.

The authorities tried in vain to drown out the powerful enemy broadcasts from adjacent bases such as Manila and Okinawa. These broadcasts in excellent Japanese exercised a great influence on the minds of the people. When it became no longer possible to suppress the truth, the Army attempted to minimize the destructive power of the bomb. They mobilized the scientists who proved willing tools for hoodwinking the nation. Then the governemnt hastily drew up a note of protest to the United States and forwarded it through the Swiss government which represented our interests.

We had, indeed, too many of these unscientific scientists who did not scruple to render a mercenary service to the military. Misguided patriots as they were, they were dupes of their own deception, and the gullible nation, soothed into false security, had to pay for it later by a bitter disillusionment.

Those irresponsible men who molded public opinion so as to preserve military domination are the ones who are responsible for our present national misery. Both scientists and publicists were in fact powerful instruments in inflaming popular hatred against [**213/214**] the democratic countries and in regimenting the people into blindly supporting the war of aggrandizement. Our people were fed upon an organized propaganda designed to uphold the prestige of the chosen nation. This made them embark recklessly upon a course of wild conquest. In pursuing such a course the hard were hardened and the blind made blinder so that they might stumble on and fall deeper into the abyss of shame.

Even without the atomic bomb the United States, by continuous incendiary raids operated by her growing armada of B-29's, could easily have destroyed all our cities and towns of more than thirty thousand inhabitants by the end of September. Now, with the sudden appearance of the new weapon, it was only too apparent that the counterassault on the home front, upon which our Army relied as the last chance, was utterly impossible.

Perhaps for a while the effect of the atomic bomb could be minimized by propaganda. But the massed invasion of Manchuria by the Red Army was impossible to hide from the people. The glacial avalanche from the north stunned GHQ. They knew that the game was up. Even for our generals the combination of the atomic bomb and the Russians proved too strong.

. . . .

We did not possess any information about the progress of the American "Manhattan project" for developing the atomic weapon. We did not know that on June 1, 1945, the American authorities adopted recommendations to the effect that the bomb should be [**214/215**] used against Japan as soon as possible, without prior

[17] Official figures announced six months later listed total casualties at 306,545 (78,150 dead, 9,284 seriously injured, 13,983 missing) but this estimate is generally believed to be too low. There were 80,000 soldiers stationed there and at least half of them perished in the raid.

[18] John Hersey, *Hiroshima* (Penguin Books, 1946), p. 91.

warning as to its nature. These recommendations were based upon the fact that there was no visible indication of any weakening in our determination to fight rather than accept unconditional surrender. As we still possessed a great military force estimated at five million men, it was thought advisable to administer a tremendous shock which would carry convincing proof of the Allies' power to destroy the Japanese Empire. It was feared that otherwise we might determine to resist to the end in all areas under our control.

The final offensives against Japan had already been planned. Operation Olympic, as it was called, envisaged an invasion of the southern island of Kyushu on November 1, 1945. The island of Honshu was not to be invaded until early in the spring of 1946. These grand designs required the deployment of a vast force of at least five million. The assault by the Sixth Army on Kyushu was to have taken the form of a trident attack converging on the southern part of the island from three directions. The final invasion of Honshu, in Operation Coronet, would have been made on the Kwanto district, the plain in which lay the city of Tokyo.

All told, operations would have involved a spectacular naval force of 3,053 vessels. In fact, the United States had by this time concentrated more than 90 per cent of her warships and 42 per cent of her combat planes in the Pacific theater. This eloquently demonstrates the magnitude of the task of invading Japan.

Allied casualties would have reached frightful dimensions if a landing had been attempted on our mainland. In Europe the casualties in the first three weeks after the Normandy landing were about 60,000 as contrasted with a monthly average of about 27,000 for the entire war.[20]

We now know that Secretary of War Henry L. Stimson on July 2 submitted to President Truman an important memorandum, generally agreed upon with Acting Secretary of State Grew and Secretary of the Navy Forrestal.[21] It said that if the Allies invaded one of our main islands in actual occupation it would most probably have "cast the die of a last ditch resistance" on our part. The Allies would then have to go through with a fight to a finish even more bitter than that with Germany, incurring a frightful loss of **[215/216]** life. For an attempt to exterminate our people by gunfire or other means, it observed, would only "tend to produce a fusion of race solidarity and antipathy which has no analogy in the case of Germany." Japan therefore should be given a warning of what was to come, accompanied by a definite opportunity to capitulate. Such a warning must be tendered before the actual invasion started.

It seems that the Stimson memorandum provided ideas which were later incorporated in the Potsdam proclamation. Stimson even suggested the inclusion in the proposed warning of the assurance that the Allies did not exclude the possibility of a constitutional monarchy for Japan under the present dynasty. The Potsdam ultimatum of July 21 omitted, however, all reference to the status of the Emperor.

. . . .

After the war we heard that these two bombs were the only ones then in the possession of the United States. But at that time the psychological impact of the bomb was so profound that the entire urban population became panic stricken lest a third attack follow on the heels of the second. In no time wild rumors started that a certain city was marked as the next victim, causing an exodus from the area in question. **[216/217]**

. . . .

One of the first questions asked me by the American war correspondents who swarmed into Tokyo with the vanguard of the occupation forces in September, 1945, "Was it the atomic bomb or Rus-

[20] D. D. Eisenhower, *Crusade in Europe*, p. 270; *World Almanac, 1950*, p. 738.

[21] Stimson, *op. cit.*, pp. 619-623.

sian participation in the war, that was responsible for the surrender?" That is a difficult question to answer. It will probably always remain a debatable point. But to us who knew the inner development it seems that neither of the two basically changed the course of the war. It is certain that we would have surrendered in due time even without the terrific chastisement of the bomb or the terrible shock of the Russian attack. However, it cannot also be denied that both the bombs and the Russians facilitated our surrender. Without them the Army might still have tried to prolong resistance. [**217/218**]

One of these journalists visited Hiroshima. When I asked his impression he said that "ninety-nine per cent of the visitors were agreed that the bomb should have never been used." That, too, is a point for future historians to debate.

The Political Target Under Assault*

THE UNITED STATES STRATEGIC BOMBING SURVEY was established by Secretary of War Stimson in 1944 for the purpose of studying the effects of our aerial attack on Germany. The results were to be used in evaluating air power as a military instrument and in determining future defense policies. In 1945 the survey undertook a similar study of the effects of our air attack on Japan. The survey, which consisted of over a thousand civilian and military personnel, secured Japanese records and interrogated hundreds of Japanese military officers, governmental officials, and political and economic leaders. Studies were made covering all important aspects of Japanese military and defense policies as well as the effects of allied operations on all phases of Japanese life at home, including the effects of the atomic bomb. *Japan's Struggle to End the War,* from which the following excerpt is taken, presents a summary report and evaluation of the material gathered by the survey.

From the foregoing calendar it remains first to outline the nature of the political target presented by Japan and second to assess various factors which contributed to the success of the assault on the enemy's will to resist.

A. To those who thought of Japanese resistance as typified by a fanatical Japanese soldier who fought until rooted out of his last-ditch foxhole, the possibility of forcing a surrender appeared to be remote. Our aim in the Pacific war was, nevertheless, to induce responsible Japanese leaders to admit defeat. Compelling such an admission at the earliest moment constituted the objective of our attack.

In total war the nature of the political target is linked to the political structure and the spirit of the enemy. In the case of Japan that spirit differed as between the general populace and the top ruling elements. This separation of public from leaders was an important consideration. **[9/10]** Japan had long been conditioned to oligarchic rule. Rigid police controls allowed the ideas and spirit of the leaders to form separately from those of the people. Popular morale therefore became just another factor in the reckonings of the ruling group. At the war's opening and throughout its early stages, the spirit of both leaders and people was chauvinistic, aggressive, expansionist. After the defeats at Midway, Port Moresby, and Guadalcanal, Japan went on the strategic defensive. Though her advance had been stemmed, she had won an empire and needed only to consolidate her conquest. Thereafter, under the pressure of our counter-offensive which eventually exposed her home islands to direct attack, seriously reduced her fleet and air forces, and blockaded her already inadequate economy, the early hope of victory was replaced by fear of defeat. Finally, a desperate determination to resist remained.

. . . .

B. By relating them to the narrative set forth in the first sections of this report, it is possible to treat separately the princi-

* The United States Strategic Bombing Survey, from "The Political Target Under Assault," *Japan's Struggle to End the War,* ed. Walter Wilds (Washington, D. C., 1946), pp. 9-13.

pal contributions to surrender made by various factors which bore on the terminal events of the war.

1. Blockade of Japan's sea communications exploited the basic vulnerability of an island enemy which, with inherently second-power resources, was struggling to enlarge its capabilities by milking the raw materials of a rich conquered area. Acute dependence upon imports of such basic items as oil, iron ore, coal, bauxite, food, etc., caused Japan's shipping position even in the fall of 1941 to appear deficient to several members of the Jushin, whose opinions were declared to Tojo before the Pearl Harbor attack. These fears were [**10/11**] well-founded, at least for long-term fighting, since Japan began the war with 6,000,000 tons of merchant shipping, which were barely sufficient for estimated minimum requirements. Her capacity to build was quickly exceeded by losses. Eighty-eight per cent of Japan's total merchant shipping available during the war was sunk. United States submarines sank 55 per cent of the total lost. Our Navy and Army air forces made important contributions by sinking 40 per cent of Japan's total shipping lost, by interdiction of sea routes, and by an aerial mining program carried out by B-29s in the last months of the war which sealed off the vital Inland Sea and disrupted every major home island port. The blockade prevented exploitation of conquered resources, kept Japan's economy off balance, created shortages of materials which in turn limited war production, and deprived her of oil in amounts sufficient to immobilize fleet and air units and to impair training. These effects were intimately associated with the political conditions culminating in the fall of Tojo and Koiso. The direct military and economic limitations imposed by shortages created virtually insoluble political as well as economic problems in attempting to achieve war production adequate for the defense of Japan. The special feeling of vulnerability to blockade, to which a dependent island people are ever subject, increased and dramatized, especially to the leaders, the hopelessness of their position and favored the growing conviction that the defeat was inevitable.

2. While the blockade was definitive in strangling Japan's war mobilization and production, it cannot be considered separately from the pressure of our concurrent military operations, with which it formed a shears that scissored Japan's military potential into an ineffectual remnant. In the early engagements that stemmed the Japanese advance and in the subsequent battle for bases, the application of our air power against vital forces which Japan committed piecemeal in defense of these perimeter positions enabled us largely to destroy her navy and reduce her air forces to impotence before the home islands could be brought under direct air attack. Throughout these operations we were employing air power effectively and potently in ways the Japanese leaders understood and feared, and had no adequate defense to withstand. Although a core of bitter-end resistance lay in Japan's army and navy until the Imperial rescript was signed, it should be noted that Tojo's collapse and the introduction of peace-making factions into the succeeding Koiso government quickly followed the loss of Saipan in July 1944. Also, after the costly and vitiating defeats in the Palaus, Philippines, and at Iwo Jima, Koiso was in turn succeeded shortly after our Okinawa landings of 1 April 1945 by the Suzuki cabinet, which was formed with the specific mandate to terminate the war. In these campaigns, dictated by our need for air mastery and won by immediate air control, while Japan's loss of effective naval and land-based air forces was overwhelming, her military attrition was not complete, since our operations used up by no means all of her ground and Kamikaze forces. Japans' principal land armies were in fact never defeated, a consideration which also supported the military's continued last-ditch resistance to the surrender decision. It nevertheless appears that after

the loss of the Marianas in July-August 1944, the military commands, though unconvinced of final victory, viewed defense against our subsequent operations as affording an opportunity for only a limited success, a tactical victory which might, so they hoped, have created a purchase from which to try for a negotiated peace under terms more favorable than unconditional surrender.

3. Fear of home island bombing was persuasive to the political leaders even before its direct effects could be felt. News of the B-29 and its intended capabilities reached Japan in 1943. B-29 raids on Kyushu and southern Honshu targets began from China bases on 15 June 1944. With the loss of Saipan in early July 1944, many leaders became wholly convinced of Japan's eventual defeat, one factor being that from Marianas bases the homeland would be brought under the kind of intensive, shattering air assault even then being administered to their German partner. The timing of the strategic bombing attack affected its role in the surrender decision. After the Marianas were lost but before the first attacks were flown in November 1944, Tojo had been unseated and peacemakers introduced into the Government as prominent elements. The war economy had already passed its peak, fleet and air forces had been critically weakened, confidence of the "intelligentsia" in the Government and the military had been deflated, and confidence by the people in eventual victory was weakening. By mid-1944 shortages of food and civilian supplies were reflected in reduced living standards. Therefore the actual physical destruction wrought by strategic bombing assumed the role of an accelerator, to assist and **[11/12]** expedite forces already in motion. It added a tremendous quantitative weight to those forces. Since the means of resisting direct air attacks had already been largely destroyed, it represented the full exploitation of air control by an air weapon. These attacks became definitive in the surrender decision because they broadened the realization of defeat by bringing it home to the people and dramatized to the whole nation what the small peace party already knew. They proved day in and day out, and night after night, that the United States did control the air and could exploit it. They lowered morale by demonstrating the disadvantages of total war directly, added a vital increment of both actual and clearly forseeable future production loss by both precision and area attacks, and applied pressure on the surrender decision by eliminating the hope of successful final resistance.

4. When Japan was defeated without invasion, a recurrent question arose as to what effect the threat of a home-island invasion had had upon the surrender decision. It was contended that the threat of invasion, if not the actual operation, was a requirement to induce acceptance of the surrender terms. On this tangled issue the evidence and hindsight are clear. The fact is, of course, that Japan did surrender without invasion, and with its principal armies intact. Testimony before the Survey shows that the expected "violation of the sacred homeland" raised few fears which expedited the decision to surrender beforehand. Government and Imperial household leaders felt some concern for the "destruction of the Japanese people," but the people were already being shattered by direct air attacks. Anticipated landings were even viewed by the military with hope that they would afford a means of inflicting casualties sufficiently high to improve their chances of a negotiated peace. Preparation of defenses against landings diverted certain resources from dispersal and cushioning moves which might have partially mitigated our air blows. But in Japan's then depleted state, the diversion was not significant. The responsible leaders in power read correctly the true situation and embraced surrender well before invasion was expected.

5. So long as Germany remained in the war that fact contributed to the core of

Japanese resistance. Slight evidence exists that some hope was held for a long-promised German miracle weapon. A telegram received on 6 May in the German embassy at Tokyo revealed that Hitler was dead, the promised new weapon had failed to materialize and that Germany would surrender within a matter of hours. Kido believed, presumably on Japanese Army representations, that the Army would not countenance peace moves so long as Germany continued to fight. It is not clear whether this was a face-saving position, designed to avoid a prior Japanese surrender. In any case on 9 May 1945, immediately after the Nazi capitulation, General Anami, the War Minister, asked the Cabinet for an Imperial conference to reconsider the war situation. The significant fact, however, is that Japan was pursuing peace before the Nazis collapsed, and the impoverishment and fragmentation of the German people had already afforded a portent of similar consequences for an intransigent Japan.

6. The Hiroshima and Nagasaki atomic bombs did not defeat Japan, nor by the testimony of the enemy leaders who ended the war did they persuade Japan to accept unconditional surrender. The Emperor, the Lord Privy Seal, the Prime Minister, the Foreign Minister, and the Navy Minister had decided as early as May of 1945 that the war should be ended even if it meant acceptance of defeat on allied terms. The War Minister and the two chiefs of staff opposed unconditional surrender. The impact of the Hiroshima attack was to bring further urgency and lubrication to the machinery of achieving peace, primarily by contributing to a situation which permitted the Prime Minister to bring the Emperor overtly and directly into a position where his decision for immediate acceptance of the Potsdam Declaration could be used to override the remaining objectors. Thus, although the atomic bombs changed no votes of the Supreme War Direction Council concerning the Potsdam terms, they did foreshorten the war and expedite the peace.

Events and testimony which support these conclusions are blue-printed from the chronology established in the first sections of this report.

(*a*) The mission of the Suzuki government, appointed 7 April 1945, was to make peace. An appearance of negotiating for terms less onerous than unconditional surrender was maintained in order to contain the military and bureaucratic elements still determined on a final Bushido defense, and perhaps even more importantly to obtain freedom to create peace with a minimum of personal danger and internal obstruction. It seems clear however that in extremis the peace- [**12/13**] makers would have peace, and peace on any terms. This was the gist of advice given to Hirohito by the Jushin in February, the declared conclusion of Kido in April, the underlying reason for Koiso's fall in April, the specific injunction of the Emperor to Suzuki on becoming premier which was known to all members of his cabinet.

(*b*) A series of conferences of the Supreme War Direction Council before Hirohito on the subject of continuing or terminating the war began on 8 June and continued through 14 August. At the 8 June meeting the war situation was reviewed. On 20 June the Emperor, supported by the Premier, Foreign Minister, and Navy Minister, declared for peace; the Army Minister and the two chiefs of staff did not concur. On 10 July the Emperor again urged haste in the moves to mediate through Russia, but Potsdam intervened. While the Government still awaited a Russian answer, the Hiroshima bomb was dropped on 6 August.

(*c*) Consideration of the Potsdam terms within the Supreme War Direction Council revealed the same three-to-three cleavage which first appeared at the Imperial conference on 20 June. On the morning of 9 August Premier Suzuki and Hirohito decided at once to accept the Potsdam terms; meetings and moves thereafter were designed to legalize the decision and prepare the Imperial rescript. At the conclusive Imperial conference, on the night of 9-10 August, the Supreme War Direction Council still split three-to-three. It was necessary for the Emperor finally to repeat his desire for acceptance of the Potsdam terms.

(*d*) Indubitably the Hiroshima bomb and the rumor derived from interrogation of an American prisoner (B-29 pilot) who stated that an atom bomb attack on Tokyo was scheduled for 12 August introduced urgency in the minds of the Government and magnified the pressure behind its moves to end the war.

7. The sequence of events just recited also defines the effect of Russia's entry into the Pacific war on 8 August 1945. Coming 2 days after the Hiroshima bomb, the move neither defeated Japan nor materially hastened the acceptance of surrender nor changed the votes of the Surpeme War Direction Council. Negotiation for Russia to intercede began the forepart of May 1945 in both Tokyo and Moscow. Konoye, the intended emissary to the Soviets, stated to the Survey that while ostensibly he was to negotiate, he received direct and secret instructions from the Emperor to secure peace at any price, notwithstanding its severity. Sakomizu, the chief cabinet secretary, alleged that while awaiting the Russian answer on mediation, Suzuki and Togo decided that were it negative direct overtures would be made to the United States. Efforts toward peace through the Russians, forestalled by the imminent departure of Stalin and Molotov for Potsdam, were answered by the Red Army's advance into Manchuria. The Kwantung army, already weakened by diversion of its units and logistics to bolster island defenses in the South and written off for the defense of Japan proper, faced inescapable defeat.

There is little point in attempting more precisely to impute Japan's unconditional surrender to any one of the numerous causes which jointly and cumulatively were responsible for Japan's disaster. Concerning the absoluteness of her defeat there can be no doubt. The time lapse between military impotence and political acceptance of the inevitable might have been shorter had the political structure of Japan permitted a more rapid and decisive determination of national policies. It seems clear, however, that air supremacy and its later exploitation over Japan proper was the major factor which determined the timing of Japan's surrender and obviated any need for invasion.

Based on a detailed investigation of all the facts and supported by the testimony of the surviving Japanese leaders involved, it is the Survey's opinion that certainly prior to 31 December 1945, and in all probability prior to 1 November 1945, Japan would have surrendered even if the atomic bombs had not been dropped, even if Russia had not entered the war, and even if no invasion had been planned or contemplated.

PART FOUR
THE BOMBING OF HIROSHIMA IN PERSPECTIVE

If the Atomic Bomb Had Not Been Used*

KARL TAYLOR COMPTON (1887-1954), atomic scientist and brother of Nobel laureate Arthur Holly Compton, was closely connected with American policy on atomic weapons throughout the later period of his life. He occupied a number of important scientific, academic, and advisory positions, including professor of physics at Princeton, president of the Massachusetts Institute of Technology, and chairman of the National Military Establishment in the Department of Defense. The following article was written by Dr. Compton after a visit to Japan at the conclusion of the war.

About a week after V-J Day I was one of a small group of scientists and engineers interrogating an intelligent, well-informed Japanese Army officer in Yokohama. We asked him what, in his opinion, would have been the next major move if the war had continued. He replied: "You would probably have tried to invade our homeland with a landing operation on Kyushu about November 1. I think the attack would have been made on such and such beaches."

"Could you have repelled this landing?" we asked, and he answered: "It would have been a very desperate fight, but I do not think we could have stopped you."

"What would have happened then?" we asked.

He replied: "We would have kept on fighting until all Japanese were killed, but we would not have been defeated," by which he meant that they would not have been disgraced by surrender.

It is easy now, after the event, to look back and say that Japan was already a beaten nation, and to ask what therefore was the justification for the use of the atomic bomb to kill so many thousands of helpless Japanese in this inhuman way; furthermore, should we not better have kept it to ourselves as a secret weapon for future use, if necessary? This argument has been advanced often, but it seems to me utterly fallacious.

I had, perhaps, an unusual opportunity to know the pertinent facts from several angles, yet I was without responsibility for any of the decisions. I can therefore speak without doing so defensively. While my role in the atomic bomb development was a very minor one, I was a member of the group called together by Secretary of War Stimson to assist him in plans for its test, use, and subsequent handling. Then, shortly before Hiroshima, I became attached to General MacArthur in Manila, and lived for two months with his staff. In this way I learned something of the invasion plans and of the sincere conviction of these best-informed officers that a desperate and costly struggle was still ahead. Finally, I spent the first month after V-J Day in Japan, where I could ascertain at first hand both the physical and the psychological state of that country. Some of the Japanese whom I consulted were my scientific and personal friends of long standing.

From this background I believe, with complete conviction, that the use of the atomic bomb saved hundreds of thousands —perhaps several millions—of lives, both

* Karl T. Compton, "If the Atomic Bomb Had Not Been Used," *The Atlantic Monthly,* CLXXVIII (December, 1946), 54-56. Reprinted by permission of Mrs. Compton.

American and Japanese; that without its use the war would have continued for many months; that no one of good conscience knowing, as Secretary Stimson and the Chiefs of Staff did, what was probably ahead and what the atomic bomb might accomplish could have made any different decision. Let some of the facts speak for themselves.

Was the use of the atomic bomb inhuman? All war is inhuman. Here are some comparisons of the atomic bombing with conventional bombing. At Hiroshima the atomic bomb killed about 80,000 people, pulverized about five square miles, and wrecked an additional ten square miles of the city, with decreasing damage out to seven or eight miles from the center. At Nagasaki the fatal casualties were 45,000 and the area wrecked was considerably smaller than at Hiroshima because of the configuration of the city.

Compare this with the results of two B-29 incendiary raids over Tokyo. One of these raids killed about 125,000 people, the other nearly 100,000.

Of the 210 square miles of greater Tokyo, 85 square miles of the densest part was destroyed as completely, for all practical purposes, as were the centers of Hiroshima and Nagasaki; about half the buildings were destroyed in the remaining 125 square miles; the number of people driven homeless out of Tokyo was considerably larger than the population of greater Chicago. These figures are based on information given us in Tokyo and on a detailed study of the air reconnaissance maps. They may be somewhat in error but are certainly of the right order of magnitude. [**54/55**]

Was Japan already beaten before the atomic bomb? The answer is certainly "yes" in the sense that the fortunes of war had turned against her. The answer is "no" in the sense that she was still fighting desperately and there was every reason to believe that she would continue to do so; and this is the only answer that has any practical significance.

General MacArthur's staff anticipated about 50,000 American casualties and several times that number of Japanese casualties in the November 1 operation to establish the initial beachheads on Kyushu. After that they expected a far more costly struggle before the Japanese homeland was subdued. There was every reason to think that the Japanese would defend their homeland with even greater fanaticism than when they fought to the death on Iwo Jima and Okinawa. No American soldier who survived the bloody struggles on these islands has much sympathy with the view that battle with the Japanese was over as soon as it was clear that their ultimate situation was hopeless. No, there was every reason to expect a terrible struggle long after the point at which some people can now look back and say, "Japan was already beaten."

A month after our occupation I heard General MacArthur say that even then, if the Japanese government lost control over its people and the millions of former Japanese soldiers took to guerrilla warfare in the mountains, it could take a million American troops ten years to master the situation.

That this was not an impossibility is shown by the following fact, which I have not seen reported. We recall the long period of nearly three weeks between the Japanese offer to surrender and the actual surrender on September 2. This was needed in order to arrange details of the surrender and occupation and to permit the Japanese government to prepare its people to accept the capitulation. It is not generally realized that there was threat of a revolt against the government, led by an Army group supported by the peasants, to seize control and continue the war. For several days it was touch and go as to whether the people would follow their government in surrender.

The bulk of the Japanese people did not consider themselves beaten; in fact they believed they were winning in spite of the terrible punishment they had taken. They watched the paper balloons take off and float eastward in the wind, confident that these were carrying a terrible retribution to the United States in revenge for our air raids.

We gained a vivid insight into the state of knowledge and morale of the ordinary Japanese soldier from a young private who had served through the war in the Japanese Army. He had lived since babyhood in America, and had graduated in 1940 from Massachusetts Institute of Technology. This lad, thoroughly American in outlook, had gone with his family to visit relatives shortly after his graduation. They were caught in the mobilization and he was drafted into the Army.

This young Japanese told us that all his fellow soldiers believed that Japan was winning the war. To them the losses of Iwo Jima and Okinawa were parts of a grand strategy to lure the American forces closer and closer to the homeland, until they could be pounced upon and utterly annihilated. He himself had come to have some doubts as a result of various inconsistencies in official reports. Also he had seen the Ford assembly line in operation and knew that Japan could not match America in war production. But none of the soldiers had any inkling of the true situation until one night, at ten-thirty, his regiment was called to hear the reading of the surrender proclamation.

Did the atomic bomb bring about the end of the war? That it would do so was the calculated gamble and hope of Mr. Stimson, General Marshall, and their associates. The facts are these. On July 26, 1945, the Potsdam Ultimatum called on Japan to surrender unconditionally. On July 29 Premier Suzuki issued a statement, purportedly at a cabinet press conference, scorning as unworthy of official notice the surrender ultimatum, and emphasizing the increasing rate of Japanese aircraft production. Eight days later, on August 6, the first atomic bomb was dropped on Hiroshima; the second was dropped on August 9 on Nagasaki; on the following day, August 10, Japan declared its intention to surrender, and on August 14 accepted the Potsdam terms.

On the basis of these facts, I cannot believe that, without the atomic bomb, the surrender would have come without a great deal more of costly struggle and bloodshed.

Exactly what role the atomic bomb played will always allow some scope for conjecture. A survey has shown that it did not have much immediate effect on the common people far from the two bombed cities; they knew little or nothing of it. The even more disastrous conventional bombing of Tokyo and other cities had not brought the people into the mood to surrender.

The evidence points to a combination of factors. (1) Some of the more informed and intelligent elements in Japanese official circles realized that they were fighting a losing battle and that complete destruction lay ahead if the war continued. These elements, however, were not powerful enough to sway the situation against the dominating Army organization, backed by the profiteering industrialists, the peasants, and the ignorant masses. (2) The atomic bomb introduced a dramatic new element into the situation, which strengthened the hands of those who sought peace and provided a face-saving argument for those who had hitherto advocated continued war. (3) When the second atomic bomb was dropped, it became clear that this was not an isolated weapon, but that there were others to follow. With dread prospect of a deluge of these terrible bombs and no possibility of preventing them, the argument for surrender was made con- **[55/56]** vincing. This I believe to be the true picture of the effect of the atomic bomb in bringing the war to a sudden end, with Japan's unconditional surrender.

If the atomic bomb had not been used, evidence like that I have cited points to the practical certainty that there would have been many more months of death and destruction on an enormous scale. Also the early timing of its use was fortunate for a reason which could not have been anticipated. If the invasion plans had proceeded as scheduled, October, 1945, would have seen Okinawa covered with airplanes and its harbors crowded with landing craft poised for the attack. The typhoon which struck Okinawa in that month would have wrecked the invasion plans with a military disaster comparable to Pearl Harbor.

These are some of the facts which lead those who know them, and especially those who had to base decisions on them, to feel that there is much delusion and wishful thinking among those after-the-event strategists who now deplore the use of the atomic bomb on the ground that its use was inhuman or that it was unnecessary because Japan was already beaten. And it was not one atomic bomb, or two, which brought surrender; it was the experience of what an atomic bomb will actually do to a community, *plus the dread of many more,* that was effective.

If 500 bombers could wreak such destruction on Tokyo, what will 500 bombers, each carrying an atomic bomb, do to the City of Tomorrow? It is this deadly prospect which now lends such force to the two basic policies of our nation on this subject: (1) We must strive generously and with all our ability to promote the United Nations' effort to assure future peace between nations; but we must not lightly surrender the atomic bomb as a means for our own defense. (2) We should surrender or share it only when there is adopted an international plan to enforce peace in which we can have great confidence.

The Atomic Bomb—The Penalty of Expediency*

HANSON WEIGHTMAN BALDWIN (1902-   ), a graduate of Annapolis, resigned his naval commission in 1927 in order to become a journalist and military analyst. He was military and naval correspondent for the New York *Times* from 1937 to 1942, and he became military editor of the *Times* in 1942, the same year in which he won a Pulitzer Prize. In *Great Mistakes of the War,* the book from which the following selection is taken, Mr. Baldwin critically reviews a number of key wartime decisions.

. . . .

The utilization of the atomic bomb against a prostrate and defeated Japan in the closing days of the war exemplifies . . . [**88/89**] the narrow, astigmatic concentration of our planners upon one goal, and one alone: victory.

Nowhere in all of Mr. Stimson's forceful and eloquent apologia for the leveling of Hiroshima and Nagasaki is there any evidence of an ulterior vision; indeed, the entire effort of his famous Harper's article, reprinted and rearranged in his book, *On Active Service* is focused on proving that the bomb hastened the end of the war. But at what cost!

To accept the Stimson thesis that the atomic bomb should have been used as it was used, it is necessary first to accept the contention that the atomic bomb achieved or hastened victory, and second, and more important, that it helped to consolidate the peace or to further the political aims for which war was fought.

History can accept neither contention.

Let us examine the first. The atomic bomb was dropped in August. Long before that month started our forces were securely based in Okinawa, the Marianas and Iwo Jima; Germany had been defeated; our fleet had been cruising off the Japanese coast with impunity bombarding the shoreline; our submarines were operating in the Sea of Japan; even inter-island ferries had been attacked and sunk. Bombing, which started slowly in June, 1944, from China bases and from the Marianas in November, 1944, had been in- [**89/90**] creased materially in 1945, and by August, 1945, more than 16,000 tons of bombs had ravaged Japanese cities. Food was short; mines and submarines and surface vessels and planes clamped an iron blockade around the main islands; raw materials were scarce. Blockade, bombing, and unsuccessful attempts at dispersion had reduced Japanese production capacity from 20 to 60 per cent. The enemy, in a military sense, was in a hopeless strategic position by the time the Potsdam demand for unconditional surrender was made on July 26.

Such, then, was the situation when we wiped out Hiroshima and Nagasaki.

Need we have done it? No one can, of course, be positive, but the answer is almost certainly negative.

The invasion of Japan, which Admiral Leahy had opposed as too wasteful of American blood, and in any case unnecessary, was scheduled (for the southern island of Kyushu) for Nov. 1, 1945, to be followed

* Hanson W. Baldwin, from "The Atomic Bomb—The Penalty of Expediency," *Great Mistakes of the War* (New York: Harper & Bros., 1950), pp. 88-103, 113-114.

if necessary, in the spring of 1946, by a major landing on the main island of Honshu. We dropped the two atomic bombs in early August, almost two months before our first D-Day. The decision to drop them, after the Japanese rejection of the Potsdam ultimatum, was a pretty hasty one. It followed the recommendations of Secretary Stimson and an "Interim Committee" of distinguished officials and scientists, who had [**90/91**] found "no acceptable alternative to direct military use."[70]

But the weakness of this statement is inherent, for none was tried and "military use" of the bomb was undertaken despite strong opposition to this course by numerous scientists and Japanese experts, including former Ambassador Joseph Grew. Not only was the Potsdam ultimatum merely a restatement of the politically impossible—unconditional surrender—but it could hardly be construed as a direct warning of the atomic bomb and was not taken as such by anyone who did not know the bomb had been created. A technical demonstration of the bomb's power may well have been unfeasible, but certainly a far more definite warning could have been given; and it is hard to believe that a target objective in Japan with but sparse population could not have been found. The truth is we did not try; we gave no specific warning. There were almost two months before our scheduled invasion of Kyushu, in which American ingenuity could have found ways to bring home to the Japanese the impossibility of their position and the horrors of the weapon being held over them; yet we rushed to use the bomb as soon as unconditional surrender was rejected. Had we devised some demonstration or given a more specific warning than the Potsdam ultimatum, and had the Japanese still persisted in continued re- [**91/92**] sistance after some weeks of our psychological offensive, we should perhaps have been justified in the bomb's use; at least, our hands would have been more clean.

But, in fact, our only warning to a Japan already militarily defeated, and in a hopeless situation, was the Potsdam demand for unconditional surrender issued on July 26, when we knew Japanese surrender attempts had started. Yet when the Japanese surrender was negotiated about two weeks later, after the bomb was dropped, our unconditional surrender demand was made conditional and we agreed, as Stimson had originally proposed we should do, to continuation of the Emperor upon his imperial throne.

We were, therefore, twice guilty. We dropped the bomb at a time when Japan already was negotiating for an end of the war but before those negotiations could come to fruition. We demanded unconditional surrender, then dropped the bomb and accepted conditional surrender, a sequence which indicates pretty clearly that the Japanese would have surrendered, even if the bomb had not been dropped, had the Potsdam Declaration included our promise to permit the Emperor to remain on his imperial throne.

What we now know of the condition of Japan, and of the days preceding her final surrender on Aug. 15, verifies these conclusions. It is clear, in retrospect, [**92/93**] (and was understood by some, notably Admiral Leahy, at the time) that Japan was militarily on her last legs. Yet our intelligence estimates greatly overstated her strength.

The background for surrender had been sketched in fully, well before the bombs were dropped, and the Strategic Bombing Survey declares that "interrogation of the highest Japanese officials, following V-J Day, indicated that Japan would have surrendered . . . even . . . if the atomic bombs had not been dropped."[71] "Even before the large-scale bombing of Japan was initiated, the raw material base of Japanese industry was effectively undermined. An accelerated decline of armament production was inevitable."[72]

Admiral Chester W. Nimitz, in a talk to the National Geographic Society on January 25, 1946, declared, "I am convinced that the complete impunity with which the Pacific Fleet pounded Japan at point-blank range was the decisive factor in forcing the Japanese to ask the Russians to approach us for peace proposals in July.

"Meanwhile, aircraft from our new fields in the Okinawa group were daily shuttling back and forth over Kyushu and Shokoku and B-29's of the Twentieth Air Force were fire-bombing major Japanese cities. The pace and the fury were mounting and the government of Japan, as its official spokesmen have [**93/94**] now admitted, were looking for a way to end the war. At this point the Potsdam Ultimatum was delivered and the Japanese knew their choice.

"They were debating that choice when the atomic bomb fell on Hiroshima. They were debating that choice when our ships shelled installations within less than 100 miles of Tokyo. . . .

"The atomic bomb merely hastened a process already reaching an inevitable conclusion. . . ."

There can be no doubt that this conclusion of Admiral Nimitz will be the verdict of history. Militarily, we "killed" Japan in many different ways: by crushing defeats at sea and on land; by the strangulation of the blockade of which the principal instrument was the submarine; by bombing with conventional bombs. After the seizure of Okinawa—probably even before that—the blockade alone could have defeated Japan; was, indeed, defeating her. Admiral Leahy was right; invasion was not necessary.

By the time "intensive strategic bombing" of the home islands began in March, 1945, production of military supplies in Japan "was already 20 per cent below its peak." And this drop reached 50 per cent by July, 1945. Lack of steel and other minerals, and the inherent industrial weakness of Japan relative to her enemies, doomed the Japs. Japan was just too [**94/95**] weak for the war she waged; her ambitions exceeded her capacity.

"Aircraft production from 1942 on (long before either blockade or bombing had become effective) never reached a level sufficient to allow the Japanese to obtain air superiority in any of the contested areas. . . .

"Production of weapons and ammunition for ground troops was not sufficient to keep line troops supplied, to fill the long sea lines, and to maintain adequate stocks in reserve. . . .

"Motor vehicles were never in sufficient supply. . . ."[73]

In the words of a well known Japanese correspondent, Masuo Kato, who was in Washington for the Domei News Agency when the war started: "The thunderous arrival of the first atomic bomb at Hiroshima was only a *coup de grâce* for an empire already struggling in particularly agonizing death throes. The world's newest and most devastating of weapons had floated out of the summer sky to destroy a city at a stroke, but its arrival had small effect on the outcome of the war between Japan and the United Nations."[74]

It is therefore clear today—and was clear to many even as early as the spring of 1945—that the military defeat of Japan was certain; the atomic bomb was not needed. [**95/96**]

But if the bomb did not procure victory, did it hasten it?

This question cannot be answered with equal precision, particularly since the full story of the Japanese surrender attempts has not been compiled. But a brief chronology of known events indicates that the atomic bomb may have shortened the war by a few days—not more.

The day before Christmas, 1944 (two months *before* the Yalta conference), U. S. intelligence authorities in Washington received a report from a confidential agent in Japan that a peace party was emerging and that the Koiso cabinet would soon be succeeded by a cabinet headed by Admiral Baron Suzuki who would initiate surrender proceedings.[75]

The Koiso cabinet *was* succeeded by a new government headed by Suzuki in early April, 1945, but even prior to this significant change, the Japanese—in February, 1945—had approached the Russians with a request that they act as intermediary in arranging a peace with the Western powers. The Russian Ambassador, Malik, in Tokyo, was the channel of the approach. The Russians, however, set their price of mediation so high that the Japanese temporarily dropped the matter. The United States was not officially informed of this approach until after the end of the war. [**96/97**]

Prior to, coincident with, and after this February attempt, ill-defined peace approaches were made through the Japanese Ambassadors in Stockholm and Moscow, particularly Moscow. These approaches were so informal, and to some extent represented to such a degree the personal initiative of the two Ambassadors concerned, that they never came to a head.

But after a meeting with Stalin in Moscow on May 27, before the trial A-bomb was even tested in New Mexico, Harry Hopkins cabled President Truman that:

"1. Japan is doomed and the Japanese know it.

"2. Peace feelers are being put out by certain elements in Japan. . . ."[76]

In April, 1945, as the United States was establishing a foothold on Okinawa, the Russians in effect denounced their neutrality agreement with Japan, and from then until July 12, the new cabinet was moving rapidly toward surrender attempts.

On July 12, fourteen days before we issued the Potsdam Proclamation, these attempts reached a clearly defined point. Prince Konoye was received by the Emperor on that day and ordered to Moscow as a peace plenipotentiary to "secure peace at any price."[77] On July 13, Moscow was notified officially by the Japanese foreign office that the "Emperor was desirous of peace."[78] [**97/98**]

It was hoped that Moscow would inform the United States and Britain at the Potsdam conference of Japan's desire to discuss peace. But instead of an answer from the "Big Three," Ambassador Sato in Moscow was told by Molotov on August 8 of Russia's entry into the war against Japan, effective immediately.

However, since early May—well before this disappointing denouement to the most definite peace attempts the Japanese had yet made—the six-man Supreme War Direction Council in Japan had been discussing peace. On June 20, the Emperor told the (Supreme War Direction) Council that it "was necessary to have a plan to close the war at once as well as a plan to defend the home islands."[79]

The Council was deadlocked three to three, and Premier Suzuki, to break the deadlock, had decided to summon a Gozenkaigi (a meeting of "Elder Statesmen," summoned only in hours of crises) at which the Emperor himself could make the decision for peace or further war. Suzuki knew his Emperor's mind; Hirohito had been convinced for some weeks that peace was the only answer to Japan's ordeal.

The first atomic bomb was dropped on Hiroshima on August 6; Russia entered the war on August 8; and the second atomic bomb was dropped on Nagasaki on August 9. The dropping of the first bomb, [**98/99**] and the Russian entry into the war, gave Suzuki additional arguments for again putting the issue before the Supreme War Direction Council, and, on August 9, he won their approval for the Gozenkaigi. But neither the people of Japan nor their leaders were as impressed with the atomic bomb as were we. The public did not know until after the war what had happened to Hiroshima; and even so, they had endured fire raids against Tokyo which had caused more casualties than the atomic bomb and had devastated a greater area than that destroyed at Hiroshima. The Supreme War Direction Council was initially told that a fragment of the Hiroshima bomb indicated that it was made in Germany (!), that it appeared to be a conventional explosive of great power, and that there was only one bomb available. When the Gozenkaigi actually was held on August 14, five days after the second bomb was dropped, War Minister Anami and the chiefs of the Army and Navy General Staff —three members of the War Council who had been adamant for continuation of the war—were still in favor of continuing it; those who had wanted peace still wanted it. In other words, the bomb changed no opinions; the Emperor himself, who had already favored peace, broke the deadlock.

"If nobody else has any opinion to express," Hirohito said, "we would express our own. We demand [**99/100**] that you will agree to it. We see only one way left for Japan to save herself. That is the reason we have made this determination to endure the unendurable and suffer the insufferable."[80]

In the words of Harry F. Kern, managing editor of *Newsweek,* who had made a special study, with the assistance of *Newsweek* correspondents, of the events surrounding the Japanese surrender:

"I think it's fair to say that the principal effect of the atom bomb on the Japanese surrender was to provide Suzuki with the immediate excuse for setting in motion the chain of events which resulted in the surrender." (An "excuse" was necessary— as the attempted military coup, following the Gozenkaigi of August 14, showed— if the leaders of the "peace party" were to avoid assassination at the hands of the rabid militarists of the "war party.")

"However, I think it is also a reasonable surmise that the Russian declaration of war would have served the same purpose, and that the dropping of the bomb was therefore unnecessary. In no case was the dropping of the bomb the reason for the Japanese surrender, and I don't think we can say that it acted as anything more than a catalyst in advancing the plans of Suzuki and his supporters."[81]

Or, as the Strategic Bombing Survey puts it, "it is the Survey's opinion that certainly prior to December [**100/101**] 31, 1945, and in all probability prior to November 1, 1945, Japan would have surrendered even if the atomic bombs had not been dropped, even if Russia had not entered the war, and even if no invasion had been planned or contemplated."[82]

This seems, in the light of history, a reasonable judgment, and, in view of our available intelligence estimates, one that we could have then made. It is quite possible that the atomic bombs shortened the war by a day, a week, or a month or two —not more.

But at what a price! For whether or not the atomic bomb hastened victory, it is quite clear it has not won the peace.

Some may point to the comparative tranquility of Japan under MacArthur in the postwar period as due in part to the terror of American arms created by the bomb. This is scarcely so; Japan's seeming tranquility is a surface one which has been furthered by a single occupation authority and the nature of the Japanese people. But I venture to estimate that those who suffered at Hiroshima and Nagasaki will never forget it, and that we sowed there a whirlwind of hate which we shall someday reap.

In estimating the effect of the use of the bomb upon the peace, we must remember, first, that we used the bomb for one purpose, and one only: not to secure a more equable peace, but to hasten victory. By using [**101/102**] the bomb we have become identified, rightfully or wrongly, as inheritors of the mantle of Genghis Khan and all those of past history who have justified the use of utter ruthlessness in war.

It may well be argued, of course, that war—least of all modern war—knows no humanity, no rules, and no limitations, and that death by the atomic bomb is no worse than death by fire bombs or high explosives or gas or flame throwers. It is, of course, true that the atomic bomb is no worse qualitatively than other lethal weapons; it is merely quantitatively more powerful; other weapons cause death in fearful ways; the atomic bomb caused more deaths. We already had utilized fire raids, mass bombardment of cities, and flame throwers in the name of expediency and victory prior to August 6, even though many of our people had recoiled from such practices.

Even as late as June 1, 1945, Stimson "had sternly questioned his Air Forces leader, wanting to know whether the apparently indiscriminate bombings of Tokyo were absolutely necessary. Perhaps, as he [Stimson] later said, he was misled by the constant talk of 'precision bombing,' but he had believed that even air power could be limited in its use by the old concept of 'legitimate military targets.' Now in the conflagration bombings by massed B-29's, he was permitting a kind of total war he had always hated, and [**102/103**] in recommending the use of the atomic bomb he was implicitly confessing that there could be no significant limits to the horror of modern war."[83]

If we accept this confession—that there can be no limits set to modern war—we must also accept the bitter inheritance of Genghis Khan and the mantles of all the other ruthless despoilers of the past. [**103/113**]

. . . .

70 [Henry L. Stimson and McGeorge Bundy, *On Active Service* (New York, Harper & Brothers, 1948), p. 610].

71 "Air Campaigns of the Pacific War," Strategic Bombing Survey, Government Printing Office, Washington, D.C., 1947, p. 53.

72 "The Effects of Strategic Bombing on Japan's War Economy, Appendix A B C," Strategic Bombing Survey, Government Printing Office, Washington, D.C., 1946.

73 "Japanese War Production Industries," Strategic Bombing Survey, Government Printing Office, Washington, D.C., 1946, pp. 1, 61.

74 Masuo Kato, *The Lost War* (New York, Alfred A. Knopf, 1946).

75 Ellis M. Zacharias, "The A Bomb Was Not Needed," *United Nations World*, August, 1949.

76 [Robert E. Sherwood, *Roosevelt and Hopkins* (New York, Harper & Brothers, 1948), p. 903.]

77 "The Summary Report on the Pacific War," Strategic Bombing Survey, Government Printing Office, Washington, D.C., 1946, p. 26. *See also* "Japan's Struggle to End the War," same source.

78 Kato, *op. cit.*

79 *Ibid.*, p. 26, *n.*

80 *Ibid.*

81 From a letter to the author, January 5, 1949 [113/114]

82 Strategic Bombing Survey. "The Summary Report on the Pacific War" *op. cit.*, p. 26.

83 Stimson, *op. cit.*, pp. 632-33.

. . . .

The Decision to Use the Bombs*

PATRICK MAYNARD STUART BLACKETT (1897-   ), British Nobel prizewinner in physics (1948), has been noted not only for his outstanding scientific work but also for his outspoken political views, especially in connection with international control of atomic energy. In his book, *Fear, War, and the Bomb,* from which this selection is taken, Blackett criticizes the Western position on control of atomic energy and defends the Soviet position.

The origin of the decision to drop the bombs on two Japanese cities, and the timing of this event, both in relation to the ending of the Japanese war and to the future pattern of international relations, has already given rise to intense controversy and will surely be the subject of critical historical study in the future. The story has, however, great practical importance if one is to understand aright many aspects of American policy and opinion, and of the Russian reaction thereto. [**127/130**]

. . . .

Why this necessity for speed? What was it in the war plans of the Allies which necessitated rapid action? Mr. Stimson's article makes it clear that there was nothing in the American-British military plan of campaign against Japan which demanded speed in dropping the bombs in early August, 1945.

Mr. Stimson describes the American war plans as follows:

> The strategic plans of our armed forces for the defeat of Japan, as they stood in July, had been prepared without reliance on the atomic bomb, which had not yet been tested in New Mexico. We were planning an intensified sea and air blockade and greatly intensified air bombing, through the summer and early fall, to be followed on November 1 by the invasion of the southern island of Kyushu. This would be followed in turn by the invasion of the main island of Honshu in the spring of 1946. We estimated that if we should be forced to carry the plan to its conclusion, the major fighting would not end until the latter part of 1946 at the earliest. I was informed that such operations might be expected to cost over a million casualties to American forces alone.

Since the next major United States move was not to be until November 1, clearly there was nothing in the Allied plan of campaign to make urgent the dropping of the first bomb on August 6 rather than at any time in the next two months. Mr. Stimson himself makes clear that, had the bombs not been dropped, the intervening period of eleven weeks between August 6 and the invasion planned for November 1 would have been used to make further fire raids with B29's on Japan. Under conditions of Japanese air [**130/131**] defense at that time, these raids would certainly have led to very small losses of American air personnel.

Mr. Stimson's hurry becomes still more peculiar since the Japanese had already initiated peace negotiations. In his own words; "Japan, in July, 1945, had been seriously weakened by our increasingly violent attacks. It was known to us that she

* Patrick M. S. Blackett, from "The Decision to Use the Bombs," *Fear, War and the Bomb* (New York: McGraw-Hill Book Co., 1949), pp. 127, 130-132, 134-135, 137-140. Originally printed in England in slightly different form, under the title, *Military and Political Consequences of Atomic Energy* (London: The Turnstile Press, 1948), pp. 118, 119-128. Reprinted with the permission of The Turnstile Press.

had gone so far as to make tentative proposals to the Soviet Government, hoping to use the Russians as mediators in a negotiated peace. These vague proposals contemplated the retention by Japan of important conquered areas and were not therefore considered seriously. There was as yet no indication of any weakening of the Japanese determination to fight, rather than accept unconditional surrender."

On July 20, the Big Three Conference at Potsdam was in session and an ultimatum was sent to the Japanese Government on July 26. This was rejected by the Premier of Japan on July 28 "as unworthy of public notice." Unfortunately, Mr. Stimson does not give either the exact date or details of the Japanese approach for mediation through Russia, or the content of their proposals. So the exact relation between this *secret* approach for mediation and the *public* refusal of the Potsdam terms is not clear. At any rate, the reason for the immediate necessity of dropping the bomb seems no clearer.

A plausible solution of this puzzle of the overwhelming reasons for urgency in the dropping of the bomb is not, however, hard to find. It is, in fact, to be found in the omissions from both Dr. Compton's and Mr. Stimson's articles. As already shown, both give a detailed account of the future plans for the American assault on Japan planned for the autumn of 1945, and the spring of 1946. But neither makes any reference in detail to the other part of the Allied plan for defeating Japan; that is, the long-planned Russian campaign in Manchuria. We can, however, fill in this information from other sources; for instance, from Elliott Roosevelt's book, *As He Saw It,* published in September 1946.

In the chapter on the Yalta Conference (February, 1945) Mr. Roosevelt writes: "But before the Conference broke up, Stalin had once more given the assurance he had first volunteered in Teheran in 1943: that, within six months of VE day, the Soviets [**131/132**] would have declared war on Japan; then, pausing in thought, he had revised that estimate from six months to three months."

The European war ended on May 8, so the Soviet offensive was due to start on August 8. This fact is not mentioned either by Mr. Stimson or Dr. Compton in the articles from which we have quoted. The first atomic bomb was dropped on August 6 and the second on August 9. The Japanese accepted the Potsdam terms on August 14.

The U.S.S.R. declared war on Japan on August 8, and their offensive started early on August 9. On August 24, the Soviet High Command announced that the whole of Manchuria, Southern Sakhalin, etc., had been captured and that the Japanese Manchurian army had surrendered. No doubt the capitulation of the home government on August 14 reduced the fighting spirit of the Japanese forces. If it had not taken place, the Soviet campaign might well have been more expensive; but it would have been equally decisive. If the saving of American lives had been the main objective, surely the bombs would have been held back until (*a*) it was certain that the Japanese peace proposals made through Russia were not acceptable, and (*b*) the Russian offensive, which had for months been part of the Allied strategic plan, and which Americans had previously demanded, had run its course.

In a broadcast to the American people on August 9, President Truman described the secret military arrangements between the Allies made at the Potsdam Conference. "One of those secrets was revealed yesterday when the Soviet Union declared war on Japan. The Soviet Union, before she had been informed of our new weapon, agreed to enter the war in the Pacific. We gladly welcome into this struggle against the last of the Axis aggressors our gallant and victorious ally against the Nazis." [**132/134**]

. . . .

General Henry H. Arnold expressed the view[2] that "without attempting to depre-

[2] In Masters and Way (Editors), *One World or None,* p. 28.

cate the appalling and far-reaching results of the atomic bomb, we have good reason to believe that its use primarily provided a way out for the Japanese Government. The fact is that the Japanese could not have held out long because they had lost control of the air. They could offer effective opposition neither to air bombardment nor to our mining by air and so could not prevent the destruction of their cities and industries and the blockade of their shipping."

This account of the situation[3] is, of course, based on information much of which was available only after the surrender of Japan. Thus some of it, for instance, the detailed instructions of the Emperor to Prince Konoye, could not have been known to the Allied Command at the time the decision to drop the first bombs was made. It is also quite possible that in July, 1945 the Allied High Command may have genuinely misjudged the real situation in Japan and have greatly overestimated the Japanese will to resist.[4] But all this information was naturally available to Mr. Stimson and Dr. Compton when they wrote their articles justifying the dropping of the bombs.

As far as our analysis has taken us we have found no compelling military reason for the clearly very hurried decision to drop the first atomic bomb on August 6, rather than on any day in the next [**134/135**] six weeks or so. But a most compelling diplomatic reason, relating to the balance of power in the post-war world, is clearly discernible.

Let us consider the situation as it must have appeared in Washington at the end of July, 1945. After a brilliant, but bitterly-fought campaign, American forces were in occupation of a large number of Japanese islands. They had destroyed the Japanese Navy and Merchant Marine and largely destroyed their Air Force and many divisions of their Army: but they had still not come to grips with a large part of the Japanese land forces. Supposing the bombs had not been dropped, the planned Soviet offensive in Manchuria, so long demanded and, when it took place, so gladly welcomed (officially), would have achieved its objective according to plan. This must have been clearly foreseen by the Allied High Command, who knew well the great superiority of the Soviet forces in armor, artillery and aircraft, and who could draw on the experience of the European war to gauge the probable success of such a well-prepared offensive. If the bombs had not been dropped, America would have seen the Soviet armies engaging a major part of Japanese land forces in battle, overrunning Manchuria and taking half a million prisoners. And all this would have occurred while American land forces would have been no nearer Japan than Iwo Jima and Okinawa. One can sympathize with the chagrin with which such an outcome would have been regarded. Most poignantly, informed military opinion could in no way blame Russia for these expected events. Russia's policy of not entering the Japanese war till Germany was defeated was not only military common sense but part of the agreed Allied plan.

In this dilemma, the successful explosion of the first atomic bomb in New Mexico, on July 16, must have come as a welcome aid. One can imagine the hurry with which the two bombs—the only two existing—were whisked across the Pacific to be dropped on Hiroshima and Nagasaki just in time, but only just, to insure that the Japanese Government surrendered to American forces alone. The long-demanded Soviet offensive took its planned victorious course, almost unheralded in the world sensation caused by the dropping of the bombs. [**135/137**]

. . . .

Two other theories of the timing of

[3] Paul Nitze, Vice-Chairman of the U.S.S.B.S., repeated the view in the Senate Committee Hearings (Senate Resolution 179, p. 530). "It is our opinion that Japan would have surrendered prior to November 1 in any case; the atomic bomb merely accelerated the date at which Japan surrendered."

[4] It is not in dispute that had the invasion of Kyushu taken place as planned in November, and had the Japanese military forces fought as determinedly as they had previously, the American casualties would have been very heavy.

the dropping of the bomb are worth a brief notice. The first is that it was purely coincidental that the first bomb was dropped two days before the Soviet offensive was due to start. This view explains Mr. Stimson's statement, [**137/138**] "It was vital that a sufficient effort be quickly obtained with the few we had," as referring to the universal and praiseworthy desire to finish the war as soon as possible. Another variant of this interpretation is that which emphasizes the compulsion felt by many Americans to make immediate use of any new gadget, irrespective of the consequences. The difficulty about this view is that it makes the timing of the dropping a supreme diplomatic blunder. For it must have been perfectly clear that the timing of the dropping of the bombs, two days before the start of the Soviet offensive, would be assumed by the Soviet Government to have the significance which we have assumed that it, in fact, did have. If it was not intended to have this significance, then the timing was an error of tact, before which all the subsequent "tactlessness" of Soviet diplomacy in relation to the control of atomic energy pales into insignificance. That the timing was not an unintentional blunder is made likely by the fact that no subsequent steps were taken to mitigate its effects.

The second view relates, not to the timing, but to the choice of an unwarned and densely populated city as target. This view admits that there was no convincing military reason for the use of the bombs, but holds that it was a political necessity to justify to Congress and to the American people the expenditure of the huge sum of two billion dollars. It is scarcely credible that such an explanation should be seriously put forward by Americans, but so it seems to have been, and rather widely. Those who espouse this theory do not seem to have realized its implications. If the United States Government had been influenced in the summer of 1945 by this view, then perhaps at some future date, when another two billion dollars had been spent, it might feel impelled to stage another Roman holiday with some other country's citizens, rather than 120,000 victims of Hiroshima and Nagasaki, as the chosen victims. The wit of man could hardly devise a theory of the dropping of the bomb, both more insulting to the American people, or more likely to lead to an energetically pursued Soviet defense policy.

Let us sum up the three possible explanations of the decision to drop the bombs and of its timing. The first, that it was a clever and highly successful move in the field of power politics, is almost [**138/139**] certainly correct; the second, that the timing was coincidental, convicts the American Government of a hardly credible tactlessness; and the third, the Roman holiday theory, convicts them of an equally incredible irresponsibility. The prevalence in some circles of the last two theories seems to originate in a curious preference to be considered irresponsible, tactless, even brutal, but at all costs not clever.

There is one further aspect of the dropping of the bomb which must be mentioned. There were undoubtedly, among the nuclear physicists working on the project, many who regarded the dropping of the bombs as a victory for the progressively minded among the military and political authorities. What they feared was that the bombs would *not* be dropped in the war against Japan, but that the attempt would be made to keep their existence secret and that a stock pile would be built up for an eventual war with Russia. To those who feared intensely this latter possible outcome, the dropping of the bombs and the publicity that resulted appeared, not unplausibly, as far the lesser evil. Probably those whose thoughts were on these lines did not reckon that the bombs would be dropped on crowded cities.

The motive behind the choice of targets remains obscure. President Truman stated on August 9, 1945: "The world will note that the first atomic bomb was dropped on Hiroshima, a military base. That was because we wished in the first instance to avoid, in so far as possible, the killing of civilians." On the other hand, in the official Bombing Survey Report we read: "Hiroshima and Nagasaki were chosen as targets because of their concentration of activities and population." There seem here signs of a lack of departmental co-ordination.

So we may conclude that the dropping of the atomic bombs was not so much the last military act of the second World War, as the first major operation of the cold diplomatic war with Russia now in progress. The fact, however, that the realistic objectives in the field of *Macht-Politik,* so well achieved by the timing of the bomb, did not square with the advertised objective of saving "untold numbers" of American lives, produced an intense inner psychological conflict in the minds of many English and American people who knew, or suspected, some of the real facts. This con- **[139/140]** flict was particularly intense in the minds of the atomic scientists themselves, who rightly felt a deep responsibility at seeing their brilliant scientific work used in this way. The realization that their work had been used to achieve a diplomatic victory in relation to the power politics of the post-war world, rather than to save American lives, was clearly too disturbing to many of them to be consciously admitted. To allay their own doubts, many came to believe that the dropping of the bombs had in fact saved a million lives. It thus came about that those people who possessed the strongest emotional drive to save the world from the results of future atomic bombs, had in general a very distorted view of the actual circumstances of their first use.

Dropping the Atomic Bomb: Right or Wrong?*

ROBERT C. BATCHELDER (1926-) is the associate director of the Detroit Industrial Mission. He received his B.D. degree from Yale Divinity School and was ordained to the ministry in 1956. His special fields of interest are Christian ethics, social ethics, and industrial relations.

. . . .

10. IMMEDIATE REACTIONS

Was it right or wrong to drop the atomic bombs on Japan? The questions that scientists, soldiers, and statesmen had debated in whispered secrecy were shouted from the housetops after Hiroshima. The spectacular advent of the atomic bomb, and its apparent bringing of the war to a prompt close, aroused widespread public interest throughout America in atomic energy and in the ethical problems it raised. The atomic bomb became a public issue—and, inevitably, a subject for public opinion polls. In December 1945 *Fortune* Magazine published the results of a public-opinion survey in which people were asked to describe their feelings about America's use of the bomb against Japan. The alternatives posed and the results were as follows:[1]

Alternatives	*Per Cent Responding*
1. We should not have used any atomic bombs at all.	4.5
2. We should have dropped one first on some unpopulated region, to show the Japanese its power, and dropped the second one on a city only if they hadn't surrendered after the first one.	13.8
3. We should have used the two bombs on cities just as we did.	53.5
4. We should have quickly used many more of them before Japan had a chance to surrender.	22.7
5. Don't know.	5.5

So it was that only a few months after Hiroshima, fully three quarters of the American public felt our use of the bomb was [**111/112**] morally justifiable, and nearly a third of these harbored the vindictive feeling that the Japanese should have been punished even further before they had a chance to surrender. Only one person in five showed any uneasiness of conscience about our use of the atomic bomb.

The existence of a general attitude of complacency about the atomic bomb, indicated by the *Fortune* poll, was also noted by the Catholic journal *Commonweal,* which editorially decried the lack of public condemnation of the bomb's use. This was confirmed by a survey sponsored by the Social Science Research Council, which reported that within the first year of the atomic age the American public had reached a state where it "does not seem emotionally disturbed about the bomb. . . . The majority have found a way to push the bomb into the back of their minds," thus making it "possible for them to be free of active personal concern."[2]

Thus, those who were disturbed about the use of the atomic bomb—in the main, the most outspoken were churchmen and scientists—found themselves to be a small minority of the American people. Even within their own groups opinion was by no means unanimous. Many atomic scientists supported the use of the bomb

* Robert C. Batchelder, from "Dropping the Atomic Bomb: Right or Wrong?" *The Irreversible Decision 1939-1950* (Boston: Houghton Mifflin Co., 1961), pp. 111-113, 211-219, 221-222, 281, 288. Reprinted with the permission of the publishers.

against Japan and brushed aside their colleagues' conscientious scruples: "After all," retorted Enrico Fermi, "the thing's superb physics!" Yet even those who supported use of the bomb against Japan for the sake of ending the war quickly were appalled at the massive destruction of life caused by their new weapon. Fermi's wife reports that among the Los Alamos scientists a "sense of guilt" was felt "more or less deeply, more or less consciously. It was there, undeniably." J. Robert Oppenheimer, director of the Los Alamos Scientific Laboratory and the man who, more than any other, deserves credit for creation of the atomic bomb, could say, "In some sort of crude sense which no vulgarity, no humor, no overstatement can quite extinguish, the physicists have known sin; and this is a knowledge which they cannot lose."[3] [**112/113**]

The scientists' feeling of guilt did not cause them to brood over the events of the past, but rather to muster their efforts to influence the events of the future so that atomic energy would never again be used to destroy human life. Associations were quickly organized at Los Alamos, Chicago, and Oak Ridge to "urge and in every way sponsor the initiation of international discussion leading to a world authority in which would be vested the control of nuclear energy."[4] The scientists hoped that the achievement of such international control might lead to the establishment of mutual trust and peace among nations; thus their labors would result in a double benefit for mankind—not only a new source of unlimited energy, but the abolition of war itself.

Opinion was not unanimous within the churches. A few church spokesmen approved the use of the atomic bomb against Japan on the grounds that it "saved countless lives."[5] The official journal of the United Lutheran Church in America was content to leave the question of the morality of the bomb in the hands of the military, going so far as to say:

> If, as is proven, they [the atomic bombs] aided in depriving Japan of plants for the replacement of munitions destroyed in battle, or of sustenance for the population, or of such morale as is essential to a nation's continuance in combat, then adequate military reasons for employing the bomb are furnished.[6]

Others implicitly condoned the bomb's use merely by keeping silence—or by passing over the immediate moral issue to urge a return to faith so that this newest gift of science (capable of being used for good or evil) might be used in the future for the benefit of man, rather than for his destruction.

However the most vocal and influential spokesmen for the American churches, both Protestant and Catholic, either questioned the use of the bomb or condemned it outright. Although grounds for the moral judgment varied, there was a substantial consensus among leading churchmen that our use of the bomb against Japan was morally indefensible. [**113/211**]

. . . .

17. ETHICS IN THE CRUCIBLE OF WAR

. . . .

The decision to use the atomic bomb took place within a historical situation with a peculiar political-military configuration. This context shaped the way in which policymakers thought about the bomb and its relation to the war, and heavily influenced the outcome of the decision itself. In particular, the gradual acceptance of obliteration bombing as a military necessity, until the mass-bombing of Japanese cities was regarded as standard procedure, largely determined that the atomic bomb—once it was decided to use it—would be dropped on the center of a large city, despite the professed concern of our leaders to avoid the killing of undefended civilians.

This particular decision took place within a larger context, a significant characteristic of which was the tendency on the part of American leaders (both military and civilian) to think of the war in purely military rather than in political terms. As a result, the goal of the war was military victory; the way to victory was the military defeat of the enemy armed forces; since the major decisions to be made were of a military character, policy formation was delegated to military men. The result was a whole series of decisions: to treat the atomic bomb as a bigger and better military weapon, to exclude civilian leaders from the highest war councils of the nation, to accept [**211/212**] the judgment of generals that obliteration bombing was necessary for victory, to try a political method to end the war only as an afterthought, to ignore vital intelligence because it did not indicate that the enemy was ready to accept total surrender, to let a military commander decide on purely tactical grounds how much time the Japanese government should have to decide to surrender after the first atomic bomb—a series of decisions which tended to mold events in such a way that the atomic bomb would finally be used in a total and unrestrained military manner. Any one of these decisions, had the emphasis lain on the political rather than on the military way of thinking, *might* have precluded or tempered our use of the atomic bomb; the cumulative effect of making all these decisions on political rather than on military grounds could well have resulted in termination of the war by diplomatic means, and prevented the destruction of Hiroshima and Nagasaki.

Focusing more narrowly upon the specific decision to drop the atomic bomb—and taking as given the political failure and the war situation as it stood in mid-1945—one cannot escape the conclusion that the atomic bombing of Hiroshima and Nagasaki caused less loss of life (and general human suffering and chaos) than would have come about had the new weapon been withheld and the war been allowed to continue by conventional means, with or without invasion of the Japanese home islands. Within this narrow context Truman and Stimson were right: the atomic bomb did cut short the war and save thousands of lives. Nevertheless, even within the situation as it had developed by August 1945, alternatives were still open—such as a demonstration of the atomic bomb against a large military installation in Japan, followed by a stern warning—which probably would have brought about Japan's surrender without the great toll of civilian lives resulting from atomic attacks upon two large cities. [**212/213**]

II

It was noted . . . that certain of the cherished ethical principles held by scientists were transformed under the impact of the threat posed to the civilized world by Hitler's emerging power. Something of the same transformation was wrought in the ethical principles of United States leaders, both military and political, during World War II. Our Air Force had entered the war proud of its Norden bombsight, and was committed to the superior morality and military effectiveness of daylight precision bombing of purely military objectives. Our government was on record as opposed, on humane grounds, to the bombing of civilian areas. The transformation both of practice and of official justification, under the demands of "military necessity," has been documented above. Churchmen proved only slightly more resistant than political leaders to this erosion of moral principles during wartime.

Henry L. Stimson's memoirs and diary record the feelings of one who was sensitive to this transformation and resisted it, yet found himself being swept along and finally participated in it. When the B-29's began their first raids over Japan, Stimson had struck from the list of targets the cultural and religious center of Kyoto, despite the fact that it was also an important center of war industry. He believed that air power could and should be used in a limited and discriminate way—and he extracted from Robert Lovett, his Assistant Secretary for Air, a promise that the B-29's would conduct "only precision bombing" against purely military objectives. His aim, as he put it, was to maintain "the reputation of the United States for fair play and humanitarianism." But then he found that our precisely dropped bombs were falling on soldiers, civilian workers, and children alike, that flames were devouring industry, commercial districts, and private residences indiscriminately. When Stimson called in Arnold to find out "the facts" and to hold [213/214] him to "my promise from Lovett," the General told him that in the congested Japanese cities it was virtually impossible to destroy war output without also destroying civilians connected with that output. The Secretary could only say that the promise he had extracted should be honored "as far as possible."[1]

Painfully Stimson realized that

> in the conflagration bombings by massed B-29's he was permitting a kind of total war he had always hated, and in recommending the use of the atomic bomb he was implicitly confessing that there could be no significant limits to the horror of modern war. The decision was not difficult, in 1945, for peace with victory was a prize that outweighed the payment demanded. But Stimson could not dodge the meaning of his action. . . .[2]

Looking back over his five years of service as Secretary of War, he could say:

> . . . I see too many stern and heart-rending decisions to be willing to pretend that war is anything else than what it is. The face of war is the face of death; death is an inevitable part of every order that a wartime leader gives. The decision to use the atomic bomb was a decision that brought death to over a hundred thousand Japanese. No explanation can change that fact and I do not wish to gloss it over. But this deliberate, premeditated destruction was our least abhorrent choice. The destruction of Hiroshima and Nagaski put an end to the Japanese war. It stopped the fire raids, and the strangling blockade; it ended the ghastly specter of a clash of great land armies.[3]

III

Two fundamental ways of judging the morality of the use of the atomic bomb appeared during 1945 and 1946. The first was (in the broadest sense) utilitarian; the primary concern of those using this approach was the consequences of the act in [214/215] question. Will the war be shortened? How many lives will be lost? Will long-term consequences be good or evil? The method is calculative: good and evil consequences are balanced one against the other, and the right act is that which produces the most good—or, at any rate, the least evil. America's leaders used this method in determining to drop the atomic bomb on Japan. It was the choice, made with awareness of its inherent horror, of the lesser evil. Yet the results produced by this method appalled many who were disposed to follow it. Once the result was faced for what it was—the deliberate bombing of two cities, resulting in death to more than a hundred thousand, and agonizing injury to as many more—many felt that the intrinsic character of the act in itself, completely apart from any consequences stemming from it, was so clearly immoral that any ethical system justifying such an act must be bankrupt. It is impossible to predict accurately the consequences of any major decision, or to calculate good and evil results numerically. This impossibility, together with the lack of any objective moral standard by which to judge the quality of an act, means in the end that a purely calculative ethical theory will permit the plausible justification of almost any atrocity, no matter how repugnant to man's innate sense of decency.

The second basic ethical approach to the question of the atomic bombing of Japan was formalistic: it was concerned with the rightness or wrongness of the act in itself. What determines the rightness or wrongness of an act is not its consequences but its inherent quality. If the act conforms to an objective moral standard, it is permissible; if not, it is forbidden or condemned. The standard to be applied in the case of Hiroshima may be summed up in the commandment "Thou shalt not attack noncombatants directly." If an act has the form of a direct and deliberate attack upon noncombatants—no matter how many or how few, no matter what the con- [**215/216**] sequences—it is a violation of the commandment and therefore wrong.*

For example, had the atomic bomb been withheld from use, Hiroshima might have been attacked the same week by 500 B-29's dropping incendiaries; the center of the city could have been burned to the ground, with the loss of 10,000 or 20,000 civilian lives. For Roman Catholic moral theory, such an incendiary raid and the atomic bombing of Hiroshima would be on the same level of immorality. Both would equally be condemned as direct and indiscriminate attacks upon the innocent.

It may be noted, however, that despite its clarity of moral theory the Roman Catholic Church probably would not have specifically condemned such an incendiary raid upon Hiroshima in the actual situation existing in August 1945. In spite of a few lonely voices like that of Father Ford, and the often expressed concern of the Pope that aerial warfare respect the immunity of noncombatants, the fire raids had been going on regularly since March. During this time the American Catholic hierarchy had taken no forthright and united stand in opposition to mass-bombing (nor had the Protestant churches). The leading American Jesuit theologian, John Courtney Murray, later commented on the silence of the Roman Catholic Church regarding the incendiary mass-bombing attacks of World War II:

Nor was any substantial effort made [by Catholic publicists or even bishops] to clarify by moral judgment the thickening mood of savage violence that made possible the atrocities of Hiroshima and Nagaski. I think it is true to say that the traditional doctrine was irrevelant during World War II. This is no [**216/217**] argument against the traditional doctrine. . . . But there is place for an indictment of all of us who failed to make the traditional doctrine relevant.[5]

Despite the immediate clarity of moral judgment provided by the formalistic approach to ethics, it is not devoid of dilemmas. In the example just cited it is too simple, in that it would leave out of consideration the consequences flowing from the two raids. An incendiary raid on Hiroshima, like those on dozens of other Japanese cities during the summer of 1945, would have advanced the end of the war somewhat, but only imperceptibly. In contrast, the atomic raid, as we have seen, was the decisive factor that brought the war to a halt within eight days. Although in one dimension (that of form) the two raids are morally equivalent, in another dimension (that of consequences) one is morally much better than the other. To be concerned only for form and to ignore consequences is to miss much of ethical significance; for certainly it was better on moral grounds that the killing and the disruption of Japanese civil life should stop than that it should continue.

Again, let it be assumed, for the sake of argument, that Truman's estimate of the alternatives before him was accurate: it was a choice between dropping the atomic bomb on Hiroshima and proceeding with the invasion of Japan. A formalist would be compelled to judge the atomic bombing of Hiroshima as impermissible, and therefore to recommend the invasion, which would be justifiable since it would proceed by conventional and discriminate attack on the military forces of the enemy. Having accepted as justifiable the killing of 317,000 Japanese soldiers in the Philippines campaign, and the killing of 107,000 of the total garrison of 120,000 on Okinawa, the Roman Catholic position would now forbid the killing of 110,000 civilians with the atomic bomb but condone a conventional invasion even though the preliminaries and the in- [**217/218**] vasion itself took the lives of ten times that number of Japanese and Allied soldiers in

* As derived from Christian ethical theory, the proscription of direct military attack upon noncombatants is not an external limitation imposed upon a supposed right of self-defense. Rather, it roots in Christian love for neighbor which (1) imposes *as a duty* the physical restraint of an aggressor *for the sake of preventing him from harming the innocent*, and (2) at the same time prohibits direct attack upon noncombatants and the fabric of civilian life—because protection of these is the very reason for restraint of the aggressor in the first place.[4]

Manchuria, China, and the Japanese home islands. In addition, it would reluctantly "permit" the death of many civilians and the destruction of many cities from battle causes, the freezing and starvation of refugee children during the approaching winter, and the complete breakdown and disruption of the fabric of Japanese civil life—provided only that all these evils were unintended and unavoidable effects of the direct attack of the invaders upon the defenders.

It must parenthetically be stated that Roman Catholic moral theology does specify that an act right in itself (such as an attack upon enemy armed forces in a just war) is not permissible if its unintended and indirect evil consequences are of such great magnitude as to be disproportionate to the good produced by the act. Yet the principle of disproportionate evil was not applied to the invasion of Germany, which resulted in just such death, suffering, and disruption of civil life; and there is no reason to believe that it would have been the basis of Catholic condemnation of the invasion of Japan (provided that generals considered invasion a military necessity).[6]

In contrast to a moral theory that would condone the greater evil consequences, provided only that they be produced by "legitimate" means, one cannot help feeling a certain respect for the elemental morality of Truman and Stimson in their determination to avoid the massive evil of invasion if humanly possible. They realistically surveyed the situation confronting them, estimated (probably correctly) that had they refrained from using the atomic bomb the war would have continued without much change in basic character—and then resolutely chose what appeared to them to be the lesser evil, regardless of the fine points of ethical theory.

It would appear, then, that just as a purely calculative approach to ethics has no inner principle to prevent the final [**218/219**] bankruptcy of justifying an atrocity as "the lesser evil," so an ethical approach concerned exclusively with conformity to laws or norms, to the neglect of consequences, has its own peculiar form of bankruptcy. To forbid an atomic attack upon a city because of its indiscriminateness but complacently to recommend an invasion which, by "legitimate" means, would produce massive evil, death, and suffering borders on hypocrisy, or at least callousness.

The conflict between the calculative and formalistic approaches to the bombing of Hiroshima can be focused in a single question: is it right to perform an inherently immoral act in order to achieve a good end and avoid a massive evil? For the formalists the answer is easy—no, it is never permissible to do evil as a means to a good end. Considered in the abstract the problem is simple. But in a particular historical context the answer is not so simple.

The bare act of dropping an atomic bomb upon a city—considered in itself alone—is clearly immoral because it constitutes a direct attack upon noncombatants. Yet it is inconsistent to single out for condemnation the act of dropping an atomic bomb and at the same time implicitly to recommend continuation of a war that one knows will include direct attack upon noncombatants with incendiary bombs. In the midst of a historical context already compromised by past and present mass bombing of civilians, which would undoubtedly have continued in the future, can Truman justly be condemned for authorizing an atomic attack (no more and no less immoral than the fire raids) which promised to put an end to the whole badly compromised situation? [**219/221**]

. . . .

V

While it is important to recognize the ethical failures in the making of a particular crucial decision, it is even more important to be aware of the ethical failures implicit in the unquestioned assumptions about the nature of war that were shared in 1945 by American leaders and people alike. The assumptions that war is primarily a military matter, that war is now total, that the purpose of fighting a war is to achieve military victory, and that war can end in victory only if the enemy is forced to surrender unconditionally—these came to be accepted as self-evident and unquestionable truths by the vast majority of the American people, despite the fact that such axioms stand in direct contradiction to the main stream of Christian ethical thought about war. Such general assumptions about modern war were at least as important—if not more so—in the shaping of the decision to drop the atomic bomb as were the ethical considerations consciously brought to bear upon that particular choice. What is required for the future is not only that [**221/222**] proper ethical thinking be applied to the making of each particular policy decision affecting nuclear weapons. It is even more important that our whole style of thinking about war be such that these particular decisions are not—as in 1945—morally compromised before they are reached. [**222/281**]

. . . .

1 "The Fortune Survey," *Fortune*, 32:305 (December 1945).

2 Commonweal, 42:468 (August 31, 1945); Leonard S. Cottrell, Jr. (ed.), *Public Reaction to the Atomic Bomb and World Affairs* (Ithaca, N.Y., 1947), Part II, ii.

3 Robert Jungk, *Brighter Than a Thousand Suns* (New York, 1958), 202; Laura Fermi, *Atoms in the Family* (Chicago, 1954), 245; Oppenheimer is quoted in *Time* Magazine, 51:94 (February 23, 1948).

4 Fermi, *Atoms in the Family*, 245.

5 See, for example, editorial in the *Presbyterian*, 115:4 (August 16, 1945).

6 Editorial, *Lutheran*, 27:2 (August 22, 1945). [281/288]

. . . .

1 Elting E. Morison, *Turmoil and Tradition: A Study of the Life and Times of Henry L. Stimson* (Boston, 1960), 633-34.

2 Henry L. Stimson and McGeorge Bundy, *On Active Service in Peace and War* (New York, 1947), 632-33.

3 Stimson and Bundy, *On Active Service*, 633.

4 For a detailed exposition of the derivation of noncombatant immunity see Paul Ramsey, *War and the Christian Conscience* (Durham, N.C., 1961).

5 John Courtney Murray, "Remarks on the Moral Problem of War," *Theological Studies*, 20:54 (March 1959).

6 John K. Ryan, *Modern War and Basic Ethics* (Washington, 1933), 80-82; Cyprian Emanuel *et al., The Ethics of War* (New York, 1932; Catholic Association for International Peace, Pamphlet No. 9), 28-30.

. . . .

Suggested Topics for Controlled Research

The bombing of Hiroshima raises many interesting and important questions not only for students of public affairs but for every citizen. Among the questions that can be investigated thoroughly in this anthology are how the decision was reached; what alternatives were available; and whether the decision was wise; many, though not all, topics suggested below concern one or the other of them.

In examining how the decision was reached, you might consider the following groups of questions. (1) What men were involved in the decision to bomb Hiroshima? What official positions did these decision-makers occupy? How did their official positions affect their views about use of the bomb? Compare especially the views of representatives from the Army and Air Force, as reflected in the selections by Secretary Stimson and General Groves, and the views of representatives of the Navy, as reflected in the selections by Admirals Leahy and Strauss. (2) Who was consulted during the course of reaching the decision? How effectively were different viewpoints presented? What consequences did the necessity for secrecy have on the decision? Compare the statements by President Truman and Secretary Byrnes with the doubts raised by Bailey and Knebel. (3) What were the goals of the decision-makers, including goals in the war against Japan, in American relations with Russia, and in connection with domestic groups such as Congress, the military, and the scientists? Compare the viewpoints of President Truman and Secretary Stimson with the interpretations offered by Leo Szilard and P. M. S. Blackett. (4) What military and political effects was the bombing of Hiroshima expected to produce? Consult especially the selections by Secretaries Stimson and Grew. (5) What information was available to the decision-makers about Japan's ability to continue fighting, the strength of the peace movement in Japan, and the future course of the war? Consider the estimates made by President Truman, Secretary Stimson, and the military officers quoted by Admiral Strauss.

In examining what alternatives were available, you might consider these groups of questions. (1) Who among the decision-makers and their advisers recommended alternatives to dropping the bomb on Hiroshima? What alternatives did they recommend? Why? Notice especially the arguments presented in Secretary Bard's statement, contained in the selection by Admiral Strauss, and in the Franck Report. (2) What reasons were given for rejecting these alternatives? What pressures worked against the alternatives? In addition to the accounts by Secretary Stimson and Karl Compton, consult also the selection by Blackett. (3) What reasons did those scientists who opposed the decision give? Those military officers? Those state department experts? Notice the differences of opinion that existed within these groups. With respect to differences among the scientists, compare the selections by Robert Oppenheimer and Arthur Compton with the selection by Bailey and Knebel. (4) What was the main objective of the Potsdam Declaration? What was the Japanese response to it? What did the Potsdam Declaration accomplish? Consult the selection by Secretary Grew as well as the selections by Secretary Togo and Mr. Kase. (5) How accurate were the decision-makers' estimates of Japanese capabilities and intentions? Compare the statements by Secretaries Stimson and Togo, and consider the report of the Strategic Bombing Survey.

In examining whether the decision to bomb Hiroshima was wise, you might consider the following groups of questions. (1) What effects did the bombing of Hiroshima have on the course of World War II? How might the outcome of the war have been different if the bomb had not been used? Did the bombing achieve the objectives that it was intended to achieve? In addition to the selections by Secretary Togo, Mr. Kase, and Karl Compton, consult also the report of the Strategic Bombing Survey. (2) What nonmilitary consequences did the bombing have? To what extent were these consequences anticipated by the decision-makers? Consider the arguments put forth in the Franck Report and by Hanson Baldwin.

Aside from topics connected with the bombing itself, the materials collected here also enable you to consider some questions related to the nature and the study of social events generally. In the final section you found several basically different evaluations of the decision to bomb Hiroshima. Karl Compton justified the decision, Hanson Baldwin assailed it, and P. M. S. Blackett offered a controversial political explanation for it. How could three observers, after examining the same evidence, reach such conflicting evaluations? On the basis of your own examination of the evidence provided in this anthology, which of the three evaluations do you agree with? Why? Do the kinds of sources collected here provide a sufficient basis for reaching a definitive conclusion about the wisdom of bombing Hiroshima? What other kinds of evidence might be helpful? Do you think it will ever be possible to reach a definitive conclusion about the wisdom of the decision? If not, why not?

Finally, in the last selection Robert Batchelder raises important moral questions which have implications beyond the bombing of Hiroshima. On the basis of Batchelder's arguments and those of Hanson Baldwin and Karl Compton, as well as the statements by the decision-makers themselves, you might consider the following groups of questions. (1) Why was the use of an atomic bomb considered to have moral implications different from those of the use of conventional weapons? To what extent did the decision-makers consider the moral issues involved? What are the arguments one can adopt in justifying or not justifying the use of the bomb on moral grounds? Which arguments do you accept? (2) To what extent does moral blame attach to the United States for first using the weapon in the way we did? What responsibility, if any, do the citizens as a whole have for the decision? What special responsibility, if any, do the scientists have who made the bomb? The soldiers who delivered it? (3) What role *did* moral considerations play in the decision? What role, if any, *should* moral considerations play in such decisions?

Suggested Topics for Library Research

The topics for research suggested on the preceding pages can be investigated more fully with the use of supplementary materials not contained in this anthology. In addition, other related topics, not dealt with directly in this anthology, are suggested here.

In making a working bibliography for your library-research paper, you will find a number of bibliographical aids and a number of periodicals very useful. First, you should investigate the card catalog of your university or college library. Second, you should check general periodical indexes, for example, the *Readers' Guide to Periodical Literature,* the *International Index to Periodicals,* and *The New York Times Index.* Third, you should investigate bibliographies concerned especially with foreign affairs, for example, *Public Affairs Information Service, Foreign Affairs Bibliography* (in three volumes), and *Publications of the Department of State.* Fourth, you will find specialized periodicals in which there will be useful articles, for example, *American Historical Review, Atomic Information, Bulletin of the Atomic Scientists, American Political Science Review,* and *International Affairs* (London). This listing is only a sample of the variety and the number of periodicals and reference guides available for library research.

The memoirs and the biographies of decision-makers and their advisers are a primary source of information on how the decision was reached and what alternatives were recommended. The most relevant of these works have been excerpted in this anthology, but similar works can also be consulted. Among these are Walter Millis, ed., with E. S. Duffield, *The Forrestal Diaries* (New York, 1961), H. H. Arnold, *Global Mission* (New York, 1949), Ernest J. King and Walter Muir Whitehill, *Fleet Admiral King* (New York, 1952), and Dwight D. Eisenhower, *Crusade in Europe* (New York, 1948). A comprehensive account of how the decision was reached as well as how the entire atomic project was originally conceived and carried out is Fletcher Knebel and Charles W. Bailey, *No High Ground* (New York, 1960).

Although the building of the bomb was overwhelmingly an American enterprise, the atomic program was actually undertaken as a joint Anglo-American venture, and the British were entitled to be consulted before any atomic weapon was used. Since the war, some criticism has been expressed concerning the alleged breakdown of this collaboration on both the scientific and political levels. Several questions are involved. Were British scientists allowed to participate effectively in the atomic program, or were they denied necessary information? Was there genuine consultation with British leaders, or was the decision to drop the bomb in effect taken unilaterally with only formal British approval? Among the sources that throw light on these questions are Winston Churchill, *Triumph and Tragedy* (New York, 1953), Clement Attlee, "The Hiroshima Choice," *Observer* (September 6, 1959), and the exchange of letters between General Groves and Edward U. Condon in *Science,* CXXX (December 4, 1959), 1592-1600.

The most important single source for discussions of the role of the scientists in the decision to bomb Hiroshima is the *Bulletin of the Atomic Scientists,* published at the University of Chicago since 1946. Among the many articles devoted to this subject in the *Bulletin,* the most comprehensive is Alice Kimball Smith, "Behind the Decision to Use the Atomic Bomb: Chicago, 1944-45," XIV (October, 1958), 288-312. Another extensive discussion is Robert Jungk, *Brighter Than a Thousand Suns* (New York, 1958). These sources, as well as the recollections of the scientists directly concerned, suggest a number of questions for research. How did scientists differ among themselves about use of the bomb? Were scientists able to obtain a hearing for their views at the highest level of decision-making? What effects did security arrangements have on the ability of scientists to communicate with each other and with the decision-makers? The views of German scientists concerning the feasibility of developing an atomic bomb and the circumstances surrounding their decision not to attempt production of such a weapon are described in S. A. Goudsmit, *Alsos* (New York, 1947).

The story of how the bomb was built and delivered has been told a number of times. The most authoritative general account of the scientific aspects of the project is Henry De Wolf Smyth, *Atomic Energy for Military Purposes* (Princeton, 1945). A popular work relating to how the bomb was built is Daniel Lang, *Early Tales of the Atomic Age* (New York, 1948). The motivations and the experiences of the scientists who participated in the program have served as the basis for a number of works of fiction, including a novel by C. P. Snow, *The New Men* (New York, 1955). The dramatic details of how the bomb was actually delivered to its target can be found in Merle Miller and Abe Spitzer, *We Dropped the A-Bomb* (New York, 1946) and William L. Laurence, *Dawn Over Zero* (New York, 1946). What were the main scientific and technical uncertainties connected with the atomic project? How accurate were the scientists' estimates of the difficulties involved in producing the bomb and the destructive power of the weapon? What special arrangements were required to deliver the bomb to its target?

The effects of the dropping of the bomb have been widely described. A classic description of the effects on humans and property is John Hersey, *Hiroshima* (New York, 1946). Other such descriptions include Michihiko Hachiya, *Hiroshima Diary* (Chapel Hill, 1955) and Robert D. Trumbull, *Nine Who Survived Hiroshima and Nagasaki* (New York, 1957). More comprehensive descriptions of the effects of the bomb are found in several reports of the United States Strategic Bombing Survey, especially *The Effects of Atomic Bombs on Hiroshima and Nagasaki* (Washington, D.C.: 1946). The entire sequence of events leading to the Japanese surrender, including the role of the bombing of Hiroshima in hastening the surrender, has been dealt with in government documents and by several historians. The State Department, the Air Force, the Navy Department, and the Office of Strategic Services have all issued important publications concerning the surrender. The most painstaking account of the situation is Robert J. C. Butow, *Japan's Decision to Surrender* (Stanford, 1954), which also contains in an appendix the main diplomatic documents connected with the events preceding the surrender. Another excellent analysis is Herbert Feis, *Japan Subdued* (Princeton, 1961). On the basis of these sources you can investigate further the following questions. What steps had been taken by the Japanese government before Hiroshima to end the war? How much support was there in Japan for these efforts? What was the Japanese response to the Potsdam Declaration? What was the extent of the destruction inflicted upon Hiroshima? What role did the bombing have in inducing the Japanese to surrender? How significant in bringing about the surrender was the entry into the war of the Soviet Union?

Guide to Research

THE IDEA OF RESEARCH

Research is the organized, disciplined search for truth; the aim of all research is to discover the truth about something. That thing may be a historical object like the Stonehenge monuments or a historical event like the Hungarian Revolt or the Battle of Waterloo. It may be a work of literature like Shakespeare's *Julius Cæsar* or Miller's *Death of a Salesman*. It may be a recurring event like the motions of the planets or the circulation of the blood. It may be an experimentally repeatable phenomenon like behavior of rats in a maze or perception apparently unaccounted for by the five senses. Or it may be a political problem like the decision to use the atomic bomb in World War II. Archeology, history, political science, literary criticism and scholarship, astronomy, physiology, and psychology—these are some of the many divisions of research. Indeed, all the sciences—physical, biological, and social—and all other scholarly disciplines share this organized, disciplined search for truth.

The search for truth has often been confused with such aims as confirming prejudice, instilling patriotism, and praising friends and blaming enemies. The attempt to prove the preconceived conclusion *that* one college is superior to another, for example, is not research (though the attempt to discover *whether* one college is so superior is). Research is hostile to prejudice.

General Methods of Research. The best general method of research is first-hand observation. But this method is not always possible and, when it is possible, not always practical.

The best method to begin discovering the truth about something is to observe that thing and the circumstances surrounding it. To discover the truth about *Julius Cæsar* or *Death of a Salesman,* get the play and read it, or go to the theatre and watch a performance. To discover the truth about the planets, observe them through your telescope. To discover the truth about the intelligence of rats, build a maze and run some rats through it.

This first-hand observation is not always possible, however. To discover the truth about the Battle of Waterloo, you can't observe the battle. The best that you or anyone else can do is to observe other persons' observations, the recorded observations of eye-witnesses: diaries, letters, and memoirs, for instance, of soldiers and generals who were in the battle. With more recent historical events—for example, the Hungarian Revolt—you are better off. You can watch films and listen to tape recordings. You may be able to interview people who were there. But these observaations are still second-hand; and, on the whole, history can be observed only at second-hand. The sole exception is history that you have been part of. You may have fought in the Hungarian Revolt—though, if you did, you may be prejudiced.

Even when first-hand observation is possible, it is not always practical. You may have a copy of or tickets to *Julius Cæsar* or *Death of a Salesman* but not know enough about the principles of dramatic criticism to interpret the play unaided. You may have a telescope but not know how to use it or, if you do, not know what to make of what you observe through it. You may have some rats but not know how to build a maze or, if you do, not know enough about animal psychology to run your rats through it properly. The best that *you* can do under these circumstances is to supplement whatever first-hand observations you can make with observations of the first-hand observations of other people better-trained or better-equipped than you. Read *Julius Cæsar* or *Death of a Salesman* and also critics' interpretations of the play. Observe the planets, if you can, and read treatises on astronomy. Do what you can with your rats, and read reports of experiments with rats. After all, no one can master the special methods and come by the special equipment of all scholarly disciplines. Indeed, few people can do this with more than one discipline, and then not before they're thirty. But all people who want a liberal education should try to discover as much of the truth about as many scholarly disciplines as their abilities and their circumstances permit. Indeed, the achievement of this is what is meant by "a liberal education."

Primary and Secondary Sources. As the foregoing account of the general methods of research suggests, there is, ultimately, only one source of the truth about something—the thing, the event, or the phenomenon itself: the Stonehenge monuments, the Hungarian Revolt, or the Battle of Waterloo; the text of *Julius Cæsar* or *Death of a Salesman;* Robert Oppenheimer's testimony on the use of the atomic bomb against Japan; the motions of the planets or the circulation of blood; extrasensory perceptions or rats running in a maze. Such a source is a *primary* source. And, in historical research, where the thing itself (the Hungarian Revolt or the Battle of Waterloo) cannot be observed at first hand, a report of an eyewitness or a film or a tape recording is also counted as a *primary* source. But any other second-hand source (an interpretation of *Julius Cæsar* or *Death of a Salesman,* a treatise on astronomy, a report of an experiment with rats) is a *secondary* source.

A primary source is, of course, better. But, if a primary source is unavailable to you (if it is a book, perhaps your school library does not have it) or if you are not trained or equipped to use it (you don't know how to run rats through a maze or you have no telescope), then a secondary source must do. In any case, except for the most mature scientists and scholars, a good secondary source is useful and often indispensable.

It is worth noticing that being primary or being secondary is not an intrinsic characteristic of the source itself. It is, rather, a relationship that either exists or does not exist between a given source and a given topic of research. Consequently, a given source may be primary in relation to one given topic but secondary in relation to another. Two examples may serve to make this important point clear. Edward Gibbon's *The Decline and Fall of the Roman Empire* (1776-1788) is a secondary source in relation to the topic of the Roman Empire but a primary source in relation to that of eighteenth-century English prose style or that of eighteenth-century historiography. Samuel Taylor Coleridge's *Lectures on Shakespeare* (1811-1812) is a secondary source in relation to the topic of Shakespeare's plays but a primary source in relation to that of nineteenth-century principles of dramatic criticism or that of Shakespeare's reputation.

It is worth noticing also that a given source may be primary or secondary in relationship to more than one topic. James Joyce's novel *A Portrait of the Artist as a Young Man* is a primary source in relation not only to the topic of the structure of *A Portrait of the Artist as a Young Man* (and dozens of other topics on the novel itself) but also to the topic of use of the stream-of-consciousness technique in twentieth-century fiction.

THE RESEARCH PAPER

A research paper is a paper giving the results of research, the methods by which they were reached, and the sources, primary or secondary, which were used. A research paper attempts to tell the truth about a topic, and also tells how and where this truth was discovered. As we have seen, the sources of a research paper may be either written sources (literary texts and historical documents, for example) or sources of other kinds (experiments, for example). Since a research paper written in school is almost always based upon written (printed) sources, we shall here discuss only that kind. A research paper based upon written sources may be either a library-research paper or a controlled-research paper. A library-research paper is a research paper for which your search for sources is limited to those sources contained in the libraries available to you; a controlled-research paper, to those sources contained in one anthology—to those contained in this volume, for example. Here we shall emphasize the latter kind.

Finding Your Topic. The first step in writing a research paper based upon written sources, whether a library-research or a controlled-research paper, is finding a topic. We say "finding a topic" rather than "choosing a topic" because the process is more like finding a job than choosing a sandwich from a menu. Unless your instructor assigns you a topic, which he may do, you must look for one; and the one you find may not be just what you want but the best one that you can find. But, if you look long and carefully, you may find a topic that so well suits your interests, your capacities, and the time and the space at your disposal that your paper will almost surely be a success.

Finding a topic is the most important single step in writing a research paper, and the things that you should have in mind when looking for a topic are (1) your interests, (2) your capacities, and (3) the time and the space at your disposal. If you are interested in a topic, if you know something about the special methods of research that the topic requires, and if your topic is narrow enough to require no more time than you have for research and no greater development than you can give it in a paper of the length assigned you, then the paper that results will probably be satisfactory. For example, the topic of figures of speech in *Julius Cæsar* may interest you greatly. But, if it does, you must ask yourself whether you know enough about figures of speech to do research on them and, if you do, whether this topic is narrow enough. Even the topic of metaphors in the play would be too broad for most papers; metaphors in Brutus' soliloquies might be about right. In any case, before you take a topic for a paper, you should do some reading on that topic; otherwise, you won't know whether it is interesting, within your ability to handle, and within the scope of your assigned paper.

Once you think that you've found a topic, take great care in phrasing it. The best phrasing is a question or a series of closely related questions. Better than "The character of Brutus" is "To what extent is Brutus motivated by self-interest and to what extent by the public interest?" The latter is not only more narrow and more precise; it provides you with a criterion of relevance in selecting your sources. At the end of this volume, you will find a list of suggested topics, intended to call your attention to topics that might not occur to you. But these topics are suggestive rather than definitive or precise.

Finding Your Sources. Finding sources for a library-research paper and finding ones for a controlled-research paper, though different in several respects, are alike in certain others. Finding sources in the library requires knowledge of how to use the card catalogue, periodical indexes, special bibliographies, reserve shelves, and encyclopedias. Finding sources in this volume or a similar one does not. But, in either case, you must have a clear idea of what you are looking for; and you must be prepared to put up with a high ratio of looking to finding. In other words, you must have not only criteria of relevance but also a willingness to do a good deal of skimming and a good deal more of careful reading, some of it fruitless.

The basic criterion of relevance you provide by careful phrasing of your topic, a problem discussed in the preceding section. The other criteria you provide by making a preliminary or tentative outline—perhaps in the form of subtopics, perhaps in the form of questions. Such an outline is not to be used for your paper. The outline for your paper will probably be quite different and, in any event, cannot be made until after you find your sources and take your notes. This preliminary outline guides your research and, as we shall see, provides you with the subtopic headings necessary for your note-cards (see "Taking Your Notes," page v).

Making Your Working Bibliography. Once you have found a promising source ("promising" because, though it seems to be relevant, it may turn out not to be) you want to make some record of it so that, once you have completed your search for sources, you can turn back to it, read it, and, if it turns out to be relevant, take notes on it. This record of promising sources is your *working* bibliography. It is so called for two reasons: first, because you work with it as you proceed with your research and the writing of your paper, adding promising sources to it and discarding irrelevant ones; and, second, because this designation distinguishes it from your final bibliography, which appears at the very end of your research paper and contains only sources actually used in the paper. For a controlled-research paper, your working bibliography may be nothing more elaborate than a series of check marks in the table of contents of your research anthology or a list of page numbers. For a library-research paper, however, you need something quite different.

A working bibliography for a library-research paper is a collection of three-by-five cards each representing a promising source and each containing full information about that source. Once you have completed your research, written your paper, and discarded all promising but (as they turned out) irrelevant sources, this bibliography is identical with your final bibliography. Having a separate card for each source enables you to add and to discard sources easily and to sort and arrange them easily in any order you please. Eventually, when this bibliography becomes identical with your final bibliography, you will arrange sources alphabetically by authors' last names. Having full information about each source on its card enables you to turn back to it easily—to locate it in the library without first looking it up again. You find this information in the card catalogue, periodical indexes, or other bibliographical aids; or, when browsing through the shelves or the stacks of the library and coming upon a promising source, you find it in or on the source itself—for example, on the spine and the title page of a book.

If the source is a *book,* you should put the following information on the three-by-five working-bibliography card:

(1) the library call number,
(2) the author's (or authors') full name (or names), last name first for the first author,
(3) the title of the book,
(4) the name of the city of publication,
(5) the name of the publisher (*not* the printer), and
(6) the year of publication (often found on the other side of the title page).

See the example of such a card on the opposite page (note the punctuation carefully).

If the source is a *periodical article,* you should put the following information on the three-by-five working-bibliography card:

(1) the author's (or authors') full name (or names),
(2) the title of the article,
(3) the name of the periodical,
(4) the volume number,
(5) the week, the month, or the season of publication, together with the year, and
(6) the page numbers covered by the article.

See the example of such a card on the opposite page (note the punctuation carefully).

These two forms take care of the two standard cases. For special cases—such things as books with editors or translators as well as authors, books published in several editions or in several volumes, and daily newspapers—see any good handbook of composition.

860.3
J23

Jones, John A., and William C. Brown. A History of Serbia. New York: The Rowland Press, Inc., 1934.

WORKING-BIBLIOGRAPHY CARD FOR A BOOK

Smith, Harold B. "Fishing in Serbian Waters." Journal of Balkan Sports, VII (May, 1936), 26-32.

WORKING-BIBLIOGRAPHY CARD FOR A PERIODICAL ARTICLE

Taking Your Notes. Once you have found sources, entered them in your working bibliography, read them, and found them relevant, taking notes requires your exactly following a standard procedure if your notes are going to be useful to you when you come to write your paper. An extra five minutes given to taking a note correctly can save you a half hour in writing your paper. Here is the standard procedure:

(1) Take all notes on four-by-six cards. Never use notebooks, loose sheets of paper, or backs of old envelopes.

(2) Limit each note to information on a single subtopic of your preliminary outline *and* from a single source. It follows from this that you may have many cards on the same subtopic and many cards from the same source but that you may never have one card on more than one subtopic or from more than one source.

(3) On each card, in addition to the note itself, put
    (a) the appropriate subtopic heading in the upper left-hand corner,
    (b) the name of the source (usually the author's last name will do) in the upper right-hand corner, and
    (c) the page number (or numbers) of that part (or those parts) of the source that you have used in taking your note. If you have used more than one page, indicate your page numbers in such a way that, when you come to write your paper, you can tell what page each part of the note comes from, for you may not use the whole note.

(If you follow these first three rules, you will be able, when you come to outline and to organize your paper, to sort your notes in any way you please—by subtopic, for example—and to arrange them in any order you please. Such flexibility is impossible if you take your notes in a notebook. If you follow the third rule, you will also be able to document your paper—write footnotes, for example—without again referring to the sources themselves.)

(4) In taking the note itself, paraphrase or quote your source or do both; but do only one at a time, and use quotation very sparingly.

Paraphrase and quotation require special care. Anything between paraphrase and quotation is not acceptable to good writers: you either paraphrase or quote, but do nothing in between. To paraphrase a source (or part of a source) is to reproduce it in words and word orders substantially different from the original. When you paraphrase well, you keep the sense of the original but change the language, retaining some key words, of course, but otherwise using your own words and your own sentence patterns. To quote a source (or part of a source) is to reproduce it exactly. When you quote well, you keep both the sense and the language of the original, retaining its punctuation, its capitalization, its type face (roman or italic), and its spelling (indeed, even its misspelling).

Omissions and additions require special care. If, when quoting, you wish to omit some of the original, you may do so only if the omission does not change the sense of the original (never leave out a "not," for example! *and* if it is indicated by ellipses (three spaced periods: ". . ."). If you wish to add something to the original, you may do so only if the addition does not change the sense of the original (never add a "not"!) *and* it is indicated by square brackets. The most usual additions are explanations ("They [i.e., the people of Paris] were alarmed") and disclaimers of errors in the original, indicated by the Latin *"sic,"* meaning "thus" (Colombis [*sic*] discovered America in 1592 [*sic*]"). You must, of course, carry these ellipses and square brackets from your note-cards to your paper. And, if you type your paper, brackets may be a problem, for most typewriter keyboards do not include them. If your keyboard does not, you may do one of two things—either use the slash ("/") and underlining ("__" and "—") in such a way as to produce a bracket ("[" and "]") or draw brackets in with a pen. In any event, don't substitute parentheses for brackets.

In your paper, quotations no longer than three or four lines are to be enclosed within a set of quotation marks and run into your text; longer ones are to be set off from the text, without quotation marks, by indention from the left-hand margin and, especially in typewritten copy, by single-spacing. But never use either of these devices unless the language is exactly that of the original.

Your usual treatment of a source should be paraphrase; use quotation only if the

Fly-fishing Smith

Smith says that fly-fishing is a method of fishing used chiefly by wealthy Serbians and foreign tourists, that the flies used are generally imported from Scotland, and that "Serbian trout are so snobbish that they won't glance [27/28] at a domestic fly."

[Query: How reliable is the information in this rather facetious article?]

NOTE-CARD

language of the original is striking (strikingly good or strikingly bad), if it is the very topic of your research (as in a paper on Shakespeare's style), or if it is so complex (as it might be in a legal document) that you don't want to risk paraphrasing it.

Let us look at the sample note-card above. The topic of research is methods of fishing in Serbia; the subtopic that the note deals with is fly-fishing in Serbia; the source is Harold B. Smith's article "Fishing in Serbian Waters," from the *Journal of Balkan Sports* (see the second of the two working-bibliography cards on page v).

Note the subtopic heading ("Fly-fishing") in the upper left-hand corner; the name of the source, abbreviated to the author's last name ("Smith"), in the upper right-hand corner; the page numbers ("[27/28]"), indicating that everything, both paraphrase and quotation, up through the word "glance" is from page 27 and that everything after that word is from page 28; the sparing and appropriate use of quotation; and the bracketed query, to remind the note-taker that he must use this source with caution.

Writing Your Paper. Many of the problems of writing a research paper based upon written sources—organization, the outline, the thesis paragraph, topic sentences, transitions, and the like—are problems of expository writing generally. Here we shall discuss only those problems peculiar to such a paper. Two of these problems—paraphrase and quotation—we discussed in the preceding section. Two others remain: reaching conclusions and avoiding the scissors-and-paste organization.

When you come to make the outline for your paper and to write your paper, you will have before you three things: (1) your *preliminary* outline, containing ordered subtopics of your topic; (2) your working bibliography; and (3) your note-cards. These are the *immediate* results of your research; they are not the *final* results. They are only the raw material out of which you must fashion your paper. At best, they are an intermediate stage between finding your topic and making your final outline. The preliminary outline will not do for the final outline. The working bibliography will almost certainly require further pruning. And the note-cards will require sorting, evaluation, organization, pruning, and exercise of logic and common sense. All this needs to be done, preferably before you make your final outline and begin to write your paper, though almost inevitably some of it will remain to bedevil you while you are writing it. To put the matter in another way, you are, with these things before you, a Sherlock Holmes who has gathered all his clues but who has reached no conclusions from them, who has not come to the end of his search for truth. You must discard irrelevant clues, ones that have no bearing on the questions that you want answered. You must arbitrate the claims of conflicting or contradictory clues. You must decide which one of several probable conclusions is the most probable.

Once you have reached your conclusions, you must organize your paper and set forth this organization in your final outline. Organization and the outline are, of course, problems common to all expository writing. But a problem peculiar to the research paper is avoiding the scissors-and-paste organization—avoiding a paper that looks as though you had cut paraphrases and quotations out of your note-cards, pasted them in columns on paper, and connected them only with such phrases as "Jones says" and "On the other hand, Brown says." Such an organization is the result of a failure to reach conclusions (with the consequence that there is nothing but "Jones says" to put in between paraphrases and quotations); or it is a failure to see the necessity of giving the conclusions reached *and* the reasoning by which they were reached (with the consequence that, though there is something to put between paraphrases and quotations, nothing is put there, and the reader is left to write the paper for himself).

Documenting Your Paper. To document your paper is to give the source of each paraphrase and quotation that it contains, so that your reader can, if he wishes to, check each of your sources and judge for himself what use you have made of it. To give the source is usually to give (1) either the information that you have about that source in your working bibliography (except that the name of the publisher of a book is usually not given) or the information that accompanies each source in a research anthology *and* (2) the information about page numbers that you have in your notes. This information you may give either formally or informally, as your instructor decides.

Formal documentation is given in footnotes. For a full discussion of footnotes, see any good handbook (one cheap and widely accepted one is *The MLA Style Sheet*). The form of footnotes is similar to, but not identical with, the form of bibliographical entries. With these three sample footnotes, compare the two sample working-bibliography cards on page v:

[1] John A. Jones and William C. Brown, *A History of Serbia* (New York, 1934), p. 211.
[2] Harold B. Smith, "Fishing in Serbian Waters," *Journal of Balkan Sports*, VII (May, 1936), 27.
[3] Smith, pp. 27-28.

Informal documentation is given in the text of the paper, usually parenthetically, as in this example:

> Fly-fishing in Serbia is chiefly a sport of wealthy Serbians and foreign tourists (Harold B. Smith, "Fishing in Serbian Waters," *Journal of Balkan Sports*, VII [May, 1936], 27), though in some mountain districts it is popular among the peasants (John A. Jones and William C. Brown, *A History of Serbia* [New York, 1934], p. 211). The flies used are generally imported from Scotland; indeed, Smith facetiously adds, "Serbian trout are so snobbish that they won't glance at a domestic fly" (pp. 27-28).

As this example suggests, however, informal documentation can be an annoying distraction. It probably works out best in papers that use only a few sources. In such papers, there are few occasions for long first-references to sources: for example, "(Harold B. Smith, "Fishing in Serbian Waters," *Journal of Balkan Sports,* VII [May, 1936], 27)." But there are many occasions for short succeeding-references: for example, "(Smith, pp. 27-28)" or "(pp. 27-28)." Occasionally, informal documentation may be profitably combined with formal, as in a paper about Shakespeare's *Julius Cæsar.* In such a paper, references to the play might well be given informally —for example, "(III.ii.2-7)"—but references to critics formally.

How many footnotes (or parenthetical documentations) do you need in your paper? The answer is, of course, that you need as many footnotes as you have paraphrases or quotations of sources, unless you group several paraphrases or quotations *from the same page or consecutive pages of a given source* in such a way that one footnote will do for all. One way to do this grouping—almost the only way—is to introduce the group with such a sentence as "Smith's views on fly-fishing are quite different from Brown's" and to conclude it with the raised numeral referring to the footnote. Your reader will understand that everything between the introductory sentence and the numeral comes from the page or the successive pages of the source indicated in the footnote.

Making Your Final Bibliography. Your paper concludes with your final bibliography, which is simply a list of all the sources—and only those sources—that you actually paraphrase or quote in your paper. In other words, every source that you give in a footnote (or a parenthetical documentation) you include in your final bibliography; and you include no other sources (inclusion of others results in what is unfavorably known as "a padded bibliography"). The form for entries in your final bibliography is identical with that for ones in your working bibliography, given above. You should list these sources alphabetically by authors' last names or, if a source is anonymous, by the first word of its title, but not by "a," "an," or "the." For example:

BIBLIOGRAPHY

Jones, John A., and William C. Brown. *A History of Serbia.* New York: The Rowland Press, Inc., 1934.

"Serbian Pastimes." *Sports Gazette,* XCI (October 26, 1952), 18-19, 38, 40-42.

Smith, Harold B. "Fishing in Serbian Waters," *Journal of Balkan Sports,* VII (May, 1936), 26-32.

MARTIN STEINMANN, JR.